(CW00403360

This provocative and original book challenges the commonplace that contemporary international interactions are best understood as struggles for power. Eschewing jargon and theoretical abstraction, Mervyn Frost argues that global politics and global civil society must be understood in ethical terms. International actors are always faced with the ethical question: So, what ought we to do in circumstances like these?

Illustrating the centrality of ethics to our understanding of global politics and global civil society with detailed case studies, Frost shows how international actors constitute one another in global social practices that are underpinned by specific ethical commitments.

Case Studies examined include:

- The War on Iraq
- The 'Global War on Terror'
- Iran
- Human Rights
- Globalization and Migration
- The use of Private Military Companies

Global Ethics forces readers to confront their own necessary ethical engagement as citizens and rights holders in global society. Failure to understand international relations in ethical terms will lead to misguided action. This book should be read by all scholars and students of international relations as well as the general reader seeking an accessible account of the importance of ethical decisions in world affairs.

Mervyn Frost is Professor of International Relations and Head of the Department of War Studies, King's College, London. Educated at Stellenbosch and Oxford, he has held appointments at Rhodes University, the University of Natal and Kent University. His major publications are: *Towards a Normative Theory of International Relations* (Cambridge University Press, 1986), *Ethics in International Relations* (Cambridge University Press, 1996) and *Constituting Human Rights: Global Civil Society and the Society of Democratic States* (London, Routledge, 2002).

Critical Issues in Global Politics

This series engages with the most significant issues in contemporary global politics. Each text is written by a leading scholar and provides a short, accessible and stimulating overview of the issue for advanced undergraduates and graduate students of international relations and global politics. As well as providing a survey of the field, the books also contain original and groundbreaking thinking which will drive forward debates on these key issues.

1. Global Ethics
Anarchy, Freedom and International Relations
MERVYN FROST

GLOBAL ETHICS

ANARCHY, FREEDOM AND INTERNATIONAL RELATIONS

mervyn frost

Routledge
Taylor & Francis Group

LONDON AND NEW YORK

First published 2009
by Routledge
2 Park Square, Milton Park, Abingdon, Oxon OX14 4RN

Simultaneously published in the USA and Canada
by Routledge
270 Madison Ave, New York, NY 10016

Routledge is an imprint of the Taylor & Francis Group, an informa business

Typeset in Aldus Roman by
RefineCatch Limited, Bungay, Suffolk
Printed and bound in Great Britain by
TJ International, Padstow, Cornwall

British Library Cataloguing in Publication Data
A catalogue record for this book is available from the British Library

Library of Congress Cataloging in Publication Data
Frost, Mervyn.
  Global ethics : anarchy, freedom & international relations / Mervyn
Frost.
    p. cm. – (Critical issues in global politics ; 1)
  Includes bibliographical references and index.
  1. International relations–Moral and ethical aspects.   I. Title.
JZ1306.F76 2008
172'.4–dc22

2008012959

ISBN 10: 0–415–46609–1 (hbk)
ISBN 10: 0–415–46610–5 (pbk)
ISBN 10: 0–203–89058–2 (ebk)

ISBN 13: 978–0–415–46609–7 (hbk)
ISBN 13: 978–0–415–46610–3 (pbk)
ISBN 13: 978–0–203–89058–5 (ebk)

CONTENTS

Cuba essay —

Cuba essay.

Cuba essay.

ACKNOWLEDGEMENTS

I have been exploring the ways in which an engagement with ethical questions is central to understanding international relations for almost thirty years now. During this time I have incurred too many intellectual debts to list here. However, I would like to offer my special thanks to all the members of the *British Academy Network on Ethics, Institutions and International Relations* which was founded by Toni Erskine in 1999 and run by her since then. This group of scholars has provided me with a most congenial framework of criticism and encouragement. Of great use to me have been the insights of: Howard Adelman, Kirsten Ainley, Chris Brown, Kateri Carmola, Molly Cochran, Lynn Dobson, Francis Harbour, Tomohisa Hattori, Tony Lang, Catherine Lu, Cornelia Navari and Nicholas Rengger. I would also like to thank Lola Frost for the many highly productive conversations about this topic that I have had with her throughout this period. I, of course, accept full responsibility for any weaknesses that still remain in the argument presented below.

ABSTRACT

In this book I make the positive case for an ethics-centred approach to understanding international relations without confronting the vast array of theories currently to be found in the discipline of International Relations (IR). The array includes theories that are realist, neo-realist, liberal, neo-liberal institutionalist, interpretive, critical, post-modern, post-structural, Marxian, discourse-centred, feminist and philosophical-realist. In IR the encounters between these theories have become increasingly complex events in which theorists encounter one another in a debate that is ever more arcane and far removed from the questions of immediate concern to us as we participate in global affairs as producers, consumers, travellers, sportsmen and -women, soldiers and educators. The endless concern with epistemology, ontology and methodology is incomprehensible to most people and far removed from our daily lives in the international domain in which we have to decide what to do. Should we (or our sons and daughters) go to war in that country? Should we keep migrants out of our neighbourhoods, towns, countries or regions, or let them in? What should we do about threats to the global environment? In the fight against global terror, should we agree to our governments and their agencies using torture? In the face of globalizing forces should we erect tariff barriers or should we take them down? Should we seek to spread democracy to our international organizations or ought we to preserve the traditional arrangements? A complete list of the pressing questions would be a very long one. In this work I present an ethics-centred way of understanding international relations that indicates some answers to these pressing questions.

I set out as simply as I can a theory of international relations that:

- Is holist in that it assumes that we, the people of the world, are already participants in two major global social practices: global civil society and the society of sovereign states.
- Analyses these from the internal point of view, from the point of view, that is, of ourselves who are participating in them.
- Makes the case that, as participants, we can only understand our own actions and those of others insofar as we understand their ethical dimensions.
- Demonstrates this with reference to a range of contemporary international problems to do with migrants, humanitarian intervention, globalization, torture and global terrorism.
- Shows that at their core these have to be understood as presenting us with ethical problems.
- Sets out a substantive ethical theory that indicates how these may be resolved.
- Indicates how this approach leads to an analysis of global terrorism that is distinctively different to that which informs the current 'war on terror'.

INTRODUCTION

*Actors think
ethically.*

The goal of this book is to make the case that international interactions should be understood in ethical terms.[1] International actors
are generally concerned to act ethically and they take pains to point
out the ethical flaws in the actions of others. They are sensitive to
and concerned about the ethical criticisms of others. The argument is
directed against a view, widely held by adherents of a number of
different approaches to the subject, that we ought to understand
these relations in terms of struggles for power (classical realism);
the structural forces in play in the domain (structural realism and
Marxist approaches); or in terms of the so-called 'power/knowledge'
nexus that exists in various discourses constituting the field of international relations. Against these my contention is that international
interactions are always ethically informed, but that this aspect is
often hidden and not made apparent. I shall argue that bringing this
aspect of our international interactions to light provides us with a
more comprehensive, deeper and richer view of the field. Moreover,
taking what one might call 'the ethical turn' also helps us understand
the play of politics and power in a more nuanced way. Furthermore,
an ethically informed understanding gives us a good account of what

1 I prefer to use the word 'interactions' rather than 'relations' because it more
accurately reflects what happens between actors in the international domain.

is happening in international affairs and opens the way for the making of better policy choices. Part of the argument to be offered in this book is that the very act of analysing international affairs is itself an action, open to ethical evaluation. We can evaluate analyses of international affairs, such as the one presented in this book, in terms of whether they are ethical or not.

The arguments to be set out here are not primarily focused on meta-level analyses of ethics in IR which would only be of interest to philosophers, but which would have little relevance for participants in global politics. Rather this analysis puts forward what I take to be the most convincing substantive ethical analysis of our contemporary international practices. This analysis is of direct relevance to all participants in contemporary international politics.

In what follows I write as a participant in international affairs and I am directing myself to all my fellow participants in the contemporary practices of international relations. This is not a monograph directed specifically at specialists in International Relations.

THE UBIQUITY OF ETHICS IN INTERNATIONAL RELATIONS

When we participate in international affairs, as we all do in many different ways, ethical considerations manifest themselves in all the phases of our involvement. They are apparent in the way in which we characterize the international circumstances within which we find ourselves; they are manifest in the explanations we give to ourselves and others about how and why this state of affairs came to be as it is; they play a role in our determination of what lines of action are open to us given our circumstances; and they play a key role in the justifications we offer for having chosen one course of action rather than another. An example illustrates these points.[2] Consider the USA's military engagement in Iraq in 2003. Prior to launching the expeditionary force, the administration of the USA made an evaluation of the existing situation. Its evaluation was made clear in speeches and

---

2 The reader may choose any other example of an engagement in international affairs. It might be a minor one or one of major international significance.

Iraq

the example

briefings.[3] The view accepted by the administration in office at the time included an account of the recent history of the Iraqi state under its then ruler Saddam Hussein, leader of the Baathist party. The history included an account of the run-up, conduct and aftermath of the first Iraq war in 1991. Central to the account was an ethical evaluation of the non-democratic nature of the Iraqi state, the human rights-abusing policies of Hussein's government, the wrongful invasion by Iraq of the state of Kuwait and the failure to obey the legal and ethical injunction of the international community's stipulations in the post-war settlement. Crudely put, the account given portrayed Saddam Hussein and his government as the wrongdoers when judged from an ethical point of view. This ethical judgement was at the heart of the way in which the state of affairs just prior to the war was framed. Also, in the explanations given of the way things had developed after the first Gulf War, ethical propositions about the wrongdoing of Saddam Hussein's government featured prominently. In particular, regular reference was made to the ethically wrongful use he and his government made of the 'Oil for Food' programme.

If we move on to consider the USA government's consideration of the policy options it faced in Iraq, here again, ethical considerations played a key role. It is safe to assume that certain feasible options were, from the start, ruled out for ethical reasons. These would include the immediate use of maximum force, including the use of theatre nuclear weapons, the use of poison gas, the use of biological weapons and so on. These we may assume were not considered, or, if they were, were quickly turned aside. When force was contemplated the administration had to make decisions about the levels of force that were appropriate. These decisions were guided by well-known ethical constraints. For example, it was repeatedly stated that policies would be devised which would minimize collateral damage to civilians and so on.[4] There were references to just war principles. Once the war option had been chosen then, once again, we see the salience

3 See an example of a briefing from the President's Office given on 3rd March 2003 at http://www.whitehouse.gov/news/releases/2003/03/20030303-3.html.
4 As evidence consider the Vice-President's remark on 17th September 2003:

> In the battles of Iraq and Afghanistan and in other fronts in the war on terror, America's Air Force has played a crucial role, and it will continue to play a

of ethical considerations in the justifications provided for it. For example, on launching the expeditionary force into Iraq in 2003, President George W. Bush presented it as an ethical action. He and his advisors relied on a number of ethical arguments. Some were produced prior to the commencement of the war and others emerged as the campaign continued. Some were explicitly stated, others were implied. These included that Iraq was in breach of its Security Council commitments in terms of UN Security Council Resolution 687 and subsequently 1441. The former Resolution required Iraq to destroy all its weapons of mass destruction and allow UN weapons inspectors to verify that this had been done. Resolution 1441 arose from Iraq's failure to do this and it spelled out the consequences that would follow a further delay in completing these requirements. There are a number of different ethical arguments underlying this line of action. First, it rests on the requirement that states ought to keep their agreements (*pacta sunt servanda*) and especially those taken in accordance with international law. Second, the agreement itself was built on a number of ethical assumptions (many of which are embodied in international law) such as, states ought to desist from war and that entering into agreements to do this is, from an ethical point of view, a good thing. Also, underlying the assessment was the view that the UN itself is founded on a number of fundamental ethical principles and that the agreements it puts in place are good insofar as they promote these. President Bush also acted on the principle that Iraq was one of a number of states that formed what he called in his State of the Union Address in 2002 the 'axis of evil'.[5] Another ethical reason put forward was that Iraq harboured and supported international terrorists and that the international community of states had an ethical duty to oppose this – with force if necessary. These judgements themselves, of course, rest on the ethical contention that terrorism is wrong. Beyond these reasons, he referred to Iraq's history of human rights abuses. This reason, in turn, supported another which was that there was an ethical

crucial role in the battles to come. The Air Force's global reach enables us to project our power anywhere in the world within a matter of hours. Its new tactics and precision weapons help us achieve our military objectives while minimizing collateral damage.

5 29th January 2002.

requirement to bring about regime change so that a democratic state could be established to replace the tyrannous rule of the Sunni minority.[6] Over and above these ethical considerations were others, more assumed than overtly stated, to do with the sanctions regime that had been in place against Iraq since the first Gulf War. These sanctions, themselves instituted for ethical reasons (to prevent genocide by Saddam Hussein against Kurdish Iraqis), had been shown to have damaged the innocent, including women and children. This itself, then, was a supplementary ethical judgement. A continuation of this policy would have been ethically untenable. Yet the alternative also seemed ethically untenable. Simply lifting sanctions would have rewarded Saddam Hussein and his regime for their ethical wrongdoing. In order to prevent him committing genocide against his own people again, some other course of action was required. Force seemed a feasible, legitimate and above all ethical option.

Any participant in international relations seeking to understand the second war against Iraq might have strong views about which of the above-mentioned ethical reasons for going to war were the 'real' reasons for Bush's action and might have strong opinions about which were 'good' ethical reasons for war. But it is certain that, if one

---

6 A number of the ethical reasons he offered in justification of the military action are contained in the following section of a speech he gave at the Port of Philadelphia on 31st March 2003:

> Our victory will mean the end of a tyrant who rules by fear and torture. Our victory will remove a sponsor of terror, armed with weapons of terror. Our victory will uphold the just demands of the United Nations and the civilized world. And when victory comes, it will be shared by the long-suffering people of Iraq, who deserve freedom and dignity.
>
> The dictator's regime has ruled by fear and continues to use fear as a tool of domination to the end. Many Iraqis have been ordered to fight or die by Saddam's death squads. Others are pressed into service by threats against their children. Iraqi civilians attempting to flee to liberated areas have been shot and shelled from behind by Saddam's thugs. Schools and hospitals have been used to store military equipment. They serve as bases for military operations. Iraqis who show friendship toward coalition troops are murdered in cold blood by the regime's enforcers. The people of Iraq have lived in this nightmare world for more than two decades. It is understandable that fear and distrust run deep. Yet, here in the city where America itself gained freedom, I give this pledge to the citizens of Iraq: We're coming with a mighty force to

did not have some understanding of the ethical arguments for and against this policy, we would not understand the resulting war and the reasons for it at all.

Those on the receiving end of this war also justified what they did (or did not do) with reference to ethical considerations. For example, the Iraqi government claimed that Iraq had done its duty and had dismantled its weapons of mass destruction.[7] After the war it turned out that this claim was true. The government also claimed that it was not a host to international terror, implying that Iraq ought not to be punished for an ethical wrong it did not commit. It claimed that the international community was behaving unethically in instituting and maintaining sanctions against the country. It made the ethical claim that the sanctions were harming the innocent. It claimed, too, that Iraq had a right not to be subject to unwarranted interference in its domestic affairs. As a sovereign state it had a right to non-intervention.[8] Both are well-known ethical claims that states normally make for themselves.

Similarly, those not directly involved in the war, such as those many people around the world who opposed the American and British military intervention, justified their positions with regard to both ethical and legal considerations, the former always taken to underpin the latter. For example, there were many who said that the so-called 'ethical' reasons referred to above were all window-dressing used to hide more sinister (and unethical) underlying reasons to do with access to the oil resources in Iraq. The ethical argument here is that states, including the USA and the UK, are not entitled to simply pursue their own self-interest by military means. This would flout the sovereign right of the state of Iraq to control its own natural resources. Other arguments referred to the way in which the action of the USA and UK bypassed the processes of the UN. Underlying this argument is the ethical notion that states ought

> end the reign of your oppressors. We are coming to bring you food and medicine and a better life. And we are coming, and we will not stop, we will not relent until your country is free.

7 See the speech to the UN Security Council by the Iraqi Ambassador Mr Mohammed A. Aldouri on 5th February 2003, which may be found at: http://www.un.org/apps/news/storyAr.asp?NewsID=6083&Cr=iraq&Cr1=inspect#.

8 Many of these claims were made by Saddam Hussein in an interview with Dan Rather on CBS during the '60 Minutes' show, 26th February 2003.

to follow the procedures set out by the UN, especially in matters of peace and war. A further argument stressed that military means ought only to be used as a last resort and that in this case the actors had not yet reached the stage of last resort. Other means, short of violence, were still available to the international community to use against the regime to prevent genocide and human rights abuses. Looking at all these ethical arguments in the round, it is clear that not all opponents of the war were agreed on all of these ethically-based arguments for opposing the war, but it is nevertheless the case that a student of international relations who failed to understand these ethical arguments would not have understood the war at all.

The import of all of the above is that getting to grips with the ethical issues at stake in the war against Iraq is central to understanding it. This point may be generalized as follows: In order to participate in international affairs, either as an individual or as part of a collective actor (such as a state, international organization or a corporation), one has to have some understanding about what is happening around one and why. As we have seen in the example just discussed, this requires that one understands the ethical dimensions of what has gone before, the ethical dimensions of the present state of affairs, the ethical aspects of various policy options and the ethical dimensions of the means whose use is under consideration.

The points made above about the war in Iraq, and the ethical arguments for and against it, are true of most (if not all) our actions in world politics. Sometimes we confront problems that are overtly ethical. For example, as citizens in states, we are often acutely aware of the ethical dimensions of the situations in which we find ourselves. Here are some of the overt ethical concerns that beset us: We worry about the justness of going to war, in general, not just in the Iraqi case.[9] We have ethical misgivings about admitting or not admitting economic migrants to our countries. We have ethical concerns about the treatment of those detained on suspicion of being international terrorists. We are concerned about the treatment of national groups in specific states, for example, the Chechens in Russia, the Palestinians in Israel, the Québécois in Canada, the aboriginal

---

9 In all the examples given to this point in the argument, I wish merely to highlight that there is an ethical element to these problems. I am not making a case for any particular ethical position.

peoples in Australia (and many others). On a number of occasions we might well have had concerns about whether to intervene in certain conflicts on humanitarian grounds. Those of us in the states being intervened in worried about whether to support intervention into our countries or not.[10] Many ethical issues arise with regard to distributional issues globally. Some of these have been manifest in the most recent round of World Trade Organization (WTO) negotiations: Is the European Union justified in maintaining subsidies to farmers which disadvantage the farmers in Third World countries? Are Third World countries justified in maintaining current tariff barriers preventing the First World countries gaining market access to their territories?

In the same way that many international problems are articulated and understood by us as ethical problems, so, too, is it the case that we justify many of the things that we do with reference to ethical criteria. For example, decisions to grant international aid are justified by reference to ethical considerations. Disaster aid is similarly justified in ethical terms. The young who attend the rock concerts for international causes understand themselves to be ethically motivated (at least in part).

Similarly, our stances with regard to specific wars are justified in ethical terms. In the most recent wars in the Middle East, as we have seen above, justifications have been offered that referred to, amongst other things, the just war tradition, pre-emptive self-defence, self-defence, the prevention of tyranny, the promotion of freedom, the promotion of democracy and the protection of human rights. At the limit, the use of force was justified in terms of a struggle between good and evil.[11] Both in the Middle East and elsewhere actors in the international realm have referred to the sovereign rights of autonomous states and the rights of peoples to autonomy as grounds for using force. Reference has also often been made to religious rights – the right to be governed by Sharia law, for example. To refer to such a right is to make an ethical claim. It is not difficult to construe

[Handwritten margin note: A more traditional idea still rooted in ethics]

10 For example, in South Africa, prior to the end of *apartheid* there was a vigorous internal debate about whether international intervention through mandatory sanctions would be ethically justifiable or not. Similar debates are currently taking place in Zimbabwe.

11 President George W. Bush's State of the Union Address 29th January 2002.

almost all our decisions and actions in the international domain as having an ethical dimension.

It is not only in our role as citizens of states that we view and present what we do in ethical terms. As individual men and women active in international affairs more generally we understand ourselves to be ethical actors pursing ethical goals. Many of us contribute to non-governmental organizations that seek to promote the well-being of those less fortunate than we are. In doing so, we understand ourselves to be acting for ethical reasons. Many of us, as individuals, participate in protests of one kind or another directed at what we perceive to be injustices abroad, whether these be in opposition to war, to *apartheid*, to genocide, to unjust distributions and so on. When disaster strikes we, as individuals, often contribute directly or indirectly to the relief efforts that follow. Many people, for ethical and religious reasons, working through religious movements, often become involved in international good works. Others make similar use of service organizations like Rotary, Round Table and Lions to engage in international activities of a similar kind. They also promote 'good will' educational visits by young people to foreign countries. Even as tourists we encounter any number of ethical issues that call upon us to make difficult decisions. Should we buy goods from stalls and bazaars run by children? Should we visit sites of archaeological interest, even when these are located in authoritarian states? Should we visit game reserves that are situated on sites claimed by the indigenous people who wish to use the land for traditional purposes and/or who see the land as holy because their ancestors were buried there? The ethical issues listed above do not only present themselves to Westerners but face international actors worldwide whether they be Buddhist, Hindu or followers of Islam.

Furthermore, beyond the ethical dimensions of our social and political relationships, there is a persistent ethical dimension to our economic activities in the international domain. It is a truism that the economic component is a core component of every person's life. Each one of us needs to engage in some economic activity in order to live. It is now the case that ever greater proportions of our economic lives have an international dimension. At every point our international economic activities are shot through with ethical features. At the most basic level they rely on our notion of a right to own property.[12] Although property rights are often protected by law, we consider that the law of property itself has an ethical basis. Those who infringe such laws are themselves considered to be not just criminals in terms of the law but also wrongdoers in terms of widely recognized ethical standards.[13] Similarly, we all have ideas about what would count as a just distribution of economic assets and what would constitute injustice. In pursuit of our economic goals we make contracts and we consider these to be ethically binding. Those who break them, we say, have committed not merely a legal wrong but also an ethical wrong. We have developed complex sets of laws governing our economic behaviour both at home and abroad. In general, we argue that the laws that have been created are ethically sound or at least have an ethical basis. Here and there, for ethical reasons, we propose that the laws be reformed. A good example of this kind of argument is to be found in the support that we give (or that we refuse to give) to the positions taken by sovereign states in the current Doha round of the WTO negotiations.

The ethical dimension of our involvement in international relations is not merely confined to instances, such as those discussed above, where we confront problems that present themselves to us as *overtly* ethical. There is an ethical dimension to even the most run-of-the-mill instances of our engagement with international affairs. This is true even where the ethical dimension is not immediately patent but rather *implicit* in what we do. Consider the everyday business of participation in international trade, the activity of tourists or the transnational activities of tertiary educational institutions. In each of these spheres we, as actors, were we to be asked, would claim ourselves to be acting ethically. In our everyday conduct we simply take it for granted, without a thought, that in participating in these spheres of activity we are doing the right thing from an ethical point of view. But were we to be challenged, we would be ready with an answer to justify our actions on ethical grounds. So, for example, if, as international traders, we were charged with economic imperialism, we would no doubt defend our actions by referring to the ethical

---

12 Here I am not defending the international economic order which is based on notions of private property being an ethical value. I am simply describing a feature of the present economic order.

13 'Thou shalt not steal' is an ethical injunction.

case for free market arrangements. Similarly, if, as tourists, we were charged with the exploitation (or with causing the under-development) of the local population in the places that we visit, we might defend our action on developmental ethical grounds. In the case of international academic transfers we might make a defence referring to the ethical case for trans-border academic freedom. The general point is that when we act in the sphere of international relations we generally consider ourselves to be acting ethically and we are ready with arguments to rebut counterclaims on this score.

In summary, then, when we engage in international relations we frame and explain the circumstances in which we find ourselves, we choose courses of action, we justify our choices of policy and we evaluate our own performances, in terms that have as a central feature an ethical aspect. We could not make sense of any of these phases of our involvement without reference to the ethical dimensions in them. In order to participate in the international domain, then, an actor (you, me, anyone) has to be what one might call 'ethically literate'. In order to participate, one has to understand the terms of ethical debate in the practice(s) within which one finds oneself.

INTERNATIONAL ETHICS: THICK OR THIN?

What is puzzling, though, is that, in spite of the fact, as indicated above, that in our everyday engagement in the international domain we often (almost always) frame the context, and our interactions with it, in ethical terms, it is a commonplace amongst us that the ethical dimension of international politics is in some general sense 'thin'.[14] In spite of the ubiquitous use of ethical language referred to in the opening paragraphs above, many of us persist in holding to the position that ethical concerns are of minor relevance in the domain of international politics. We hold that in some sense they are less important in the international sphere than they are in other spheres of our lives, including those to do with domestic politics within states; families; tribes; clans and nations; and so on. There is a widespread perception that the ethical aspects of international

14 For accounts given by academics of the 'thinness' of ethics in the international realm see the positions of both John Rawls and of Michael Walzer (Rawls, 1993, passim; Walzer, 1994, passim).

politics are less important than other factors operative in this field. Indeed, there are some who regard the claim that ethics is pertinent to international affairs as an oxymoron.

Are there good reasons for holding to the view that the ethical constraints on international relations are 'thin'? Many consider the following reasons to be self-evident. First, we hold that, when looked at in the round, the interaction between participants in the international domain is governed more by a struggle for power than by our obedience to common ethical constraints and a pursuit of commonly acknowledged ethical goals. For example, it is often suggested that the USA interest in the Gulf is prompted more by a material interest in stable oil supplies than by an ethical concern for the human rights of the people in, for example, Iraq. This vague notion of the international being a domain of power play is taken up in a number of major academic theories to be found in, amongst other places, the disciplines of sociology, political science, international relations (IR), geography and history. Some theories within these disciplines stress the primary role played by states and their pursuit of power in this domain; others admit an important place for actors other than states, actors such as multinational corporations and international organizations. But these, too, are understood to be power-seeking. Yet others stress the primacy of social classes engaged in an epic international struggle for power, especially economic power. Common to them all, though, is the understanding that this is a domain of political struggle where politics is understood as the struggle for power.[15]

A second reason for considering the role of ethics to be 'thin' in the sphere of international relations is that we often present the domain as one within which we find ourselves confronted by a 'them' whose ethical commitments are different from ours. On this view we are, as it were, trapped, each in our own ethical community, without any overarching cosmopolitan ethicality to provide a common framework for ethical discussion between us and them. The substance of this insight has been played out in the well-known,

---

15 For a structural realist theory that stresses the importance of power play between states see Kenneth Waltz (Waltz, 1979); for a discussion of liberal theory see Dunne, 1997; and for a discussion of class theory applied to international relations see Amin, 1974.

cosmopolitan/communitarian debate.[16] Another version of this argument is to be found in the writings of those who portray our world order as consisting of a clash of civilizations or a domain of cultural conflict (Huntington, 1996). On this view we formulate our ideas about our relationship to others in ethical terms and they do the same about their relations to us, but between us there is no common ethicality in terms of which we can settle our ethical differences about what counts as a just war, what counts as the right treatment of an asylum seeker, an economic refugee and so on. At the very best there is a limited ethical consensus to help us here. This is the 'thin' raft of agreement on a minimal set of ethical standards (Paskins & Dockrill, 1979, pp. 205–206).

Third, the 'thin' notion of ethics in world affairs also stems from a widely accepted assumption that relations between states are governed by *conventional* rules agreed between them for pragmatic rather than ethical reasons.[17]

Fourth, support for the 'thin' view of ethics in international affairs is also provided by reference to the fact of regular and severe conflict between the diverse actors in international affairs. The argument seems to be that the fact of widespread conflict in some sense proves the absence of a 'thick' ethical dimension to our common life in this domain. The counter-factual seems to be that, if there were a substantial ethicality between people on the world stage, there would not be so many violent conflicts. These conflicts include conventional wars, struggles for secession, national liberation wars and the so called 'New Wars'. On this view, the fact of widespread and persistent conflict is evidence of an absence of an overarching ethical consensus. Presumably, were there a 'thick' ethicality, this would be marked by a zone of peace comparable to what we find in well-established, sovereign states.

Fifth, another factor which seems to point to the limited salience of ethics to international relations is the limited time and effort that individuals, politicians, theorists and states give to a serious and

16 On the cosmopolitan/communitarian debate see Cochran, 2000 and also Delaney, 1994.
17 Strong proponents of this point of view are to be found in the English School approach to international relations: Bull, 1977, passim, Wight, 1979, Buzan, Jones & Little, 1993.

sustained discussion of ethical questions in international affairs. Whereas time and money are expended on research into the causes of conflict, into the conditions for peace, into the structures for peaceful and sustained economic development, comparatively few resources are committed to a study of the ethical questions I mentioned earlier. Governments have in-house research teams seeking to explain and predict international developments and there are any number of private sector think-tanks and other specialized research bodies, and so on, that deal with such matters from an empirical and explanatory angle. The fact that resources are poured into these activities could be taken as supporting the claim that these are worthwhile activities. If they were not, why would people engage in them? Money feeds the 'thick' issues and allows the 'thin' ones to starve.

Finally, a sixth factor supporting the 'thin' view of ethics in international relations is found in the widespread belief that individual ethical commitments are a matter of individual choice and that, therefore, it is wrong to suppose that rational inquiry will reveal what the 'true' ethical stance ought to be for everyone. This belief, then, blocks people from considering, in any detail, arguments for and against rival ethical positions. If one's ethical stance is a personal one, then there is no point in looking for a single overarching ethical belief system applicable to all people everywhere, for all time, for, by definition, there are many different individual ethical creeds.[18] All one has to do is choose one's own.

To summarize, the reasons for accepting the role of ethics in international relations as 'thin' are: that the realm of international affairs is governed by power relations; there are many different ethical systems; that many of these are in conflict with one another; that there is no agreed-upon overarching ethic that may be used to sort out the differences between them; and that ethical choices are a personal matter.

Summary of reasons for 'thin'.

18 Ironically what is obscured in this line of thinking is that this belief that ethics is a personal matter is itself an ethical position. In other words, the view that it is wrong to prescribe an ethical position that is binding on all people is itself an ethical commitment. It is not a self-evident truth that all people should be left to decide their own ethical tastes on questions of war and peace, human rights, global justice and so on. The belief that they should be left free to do this is part of a particular ethical code, a liberal one. If we find that this view is widely held, then this is prima facie evidence that there is an internationally accepted ethicality.

The consequences that flow from accepting the 'thin' thesis are important. Most obviously, the role of ethical discussion in the solution of international conflict is taken to be limited, for, if there is but a limited morality to guide us in international relations, then there is not a lot to draw on when seeking solutions to urgent conflicts. When Zionism encounters Islam in the Middle East there is, on this view, little that can be achieved through ethical argument. We simply have to note the differences between the parties to the conflict and observe how things resolve themselves in terms of the play of politics and power. The Zionists have one view of what is ethically appropriate behaviour given the circumstances, and the Islamic actors have a radically divergent view of political ethics. Each attempts to impose its view on its rival. One could easily draw up a long list of similar examples of what appear to be intractable rival interpretations of what counts as right and wrong action that seem doomed to be played out in power politics.

The truth of the previous assertion leads to the further one that in international affairs we ought to accept that the role of power is likely to be more important than it is in spheres of activity where there is something of an ethical consensus constraining the behaviour of key actors, such as is to be found in the domain of domestic politics within sovereign states.

Building on this point, this way of understanding the international domain encourages us to draw a sharp distinction between the international domain and the domestic one. In the domestic realm, where citizens are bound together by a common legal system which is normally understood to rest on a particular ethical foundation, for example, a democratic one, there can be (and often are) profound and ongoing discussions about the ethical merits of developing the legal and constitutional order in one direction rather than another. The public philosophy that underpins the legal order can be used as a resource in this debate to generate answers to difficult legal and constitutional questions.[19] For example, democratic theory can be drawn on to discuss the merits of proportional representation as

19 Thus, when issues arise about how to regulate (or not) stem cell research within a particular state, citizens, parliamentarians and members of the government will draw on the public philosophy that informs the constitution under which they all live. In many such cases a call will be made on philosophies of human rights, and democratic philosophy.

opposed to Westminster-style, first-past-the-post-winner-takes-all systems of election. In communist states, communist theory could be used in a similar way to take on and to solve hard cases, as and when they arose. In Islamic states the source to be drawn on to solve difficult cases is the *Sharia*. Our standard stance towards the international domain is that it lacks this kind of widely accepted public philosophy underpinning its legal and institutional framework. Alternatively, if it does have such a philosophy it is a minimal one. So when ethical disputes arise about how the system might be changed or developed there is no widely acknowledged, and intellectually rich, public philosophy on which to call. On this view, when Islam confronts Western secular ideas there is nothing to do but acknowledge that this is a power struggle. As President Bush so graphically said, each person has to decide whether they are 'for us or against us'. Similarly, where traditional philosophies of certain African people based on theories of *Ubuntu* clash with the secular political philosophy widely accepted in the West, this, too, must be understood as a confrontation – a clash between incommensurable ethical positions.

A further crucial implication that flows from the 'thinness' thesis is that the widespread use of ethical language in international relations must be understood as so much hot air. Our use of ethical language on this view reveals our personal ethical choices and rationalizes our actions, but nothing more.

Finally, if we accept the 'thin' thesis, then it is clear that in this realm of confrontation between different and competing rival ethical codes there is great scope for tragic outcomes. Actors will often find themselves in situations where they are ethically required to act in ways which they know will bring disaster upon them. The ethical norms in the practices within which they find themselves may well compel them to behave in ways that will have very adverse consequences for them given that others do not have the same ethical commitments and given that, *vis-à-vis* those others, they are acting in the realm of naked power. For example, nationalist groups who are weaker than the groups ranged against them might feel themselves compelled by their nationalist ethic to enter into a war to protect their national values knowing that they are likely to lose that war.[20]

---

20 Something like this inspired the Finns to go to war with Russia in World War II.

Similar predicaments might beset religious believers in an international environment that is strongly secular. In these cases the actors can either remain faithful to the requirements of their ethical codes or they can surrender their core values for pragmatic reasons. The role of ethical argument in solving the conflict will be limited.

On the account that I have given above, the international domain appears to be one condemned to the repetition of power struggles and clashes between rival ethical positions. The main disciplines focused on the analysis of the international domain focus on just these power struggles.[21]

In the light of the above we now need to confront the following paradoxes: First, as actors in international relations, we often frame our predicaments, explain their origins, determine our policy options and justify our choices, in ethical terms, as indicated at the outset. Yet, at the same time we view the international sphere as one that is minimally organized on ethical principles but is rather characterized by ongoing struggles of power. We appear to be living a contradiction. It would seem that our regular use of ethical language is deeply hypocritical and a mere disguise for the pursuit of self-interest. Second, in spite of the ubiquity of ethical language in portraying the international domain, the disciplines that study this domain focus their lenses on the political struggles in this area. We generally find that social scientists and historians appear to be interested in what might be called the 'physics of international motion'. Their focus is on questions about the causes of events, particularly those relating to war and peace, rather than on questions about what ought to be done in this domain.[22] They focus not only on brute power but also on the

21 These include international relations, political science, political sociology, contemporary history, cultural studies, international law, business studies and so on.

22 Ironically, some of the most sophisticated theories that have emerged in recent times have declared themselves interested in ethical issues, but their interest is in the role ethics plays in the constitution of international power and the power struggles that have led to the emergence of certain ethical discourses as the dominant ones. The irony is that these theories are not interested in the ethical questions *per se* but in the power struggles that lead to their emergence and the empirical factors that influence the role they play in the constitution of the present day structures of international power. The theories that I refer to here are critical theory, post-structural theory and post-modern international theory. Critical theory has sought to show the role social theories play in constituting the social world within which we live. In particular, it seeks to show it is used to

complex and sophisticated power struggles that give (and have given) rise to certain dominant discourses. Readers of the texts written by such social scientists and newspaper pundits will have little sense of a sustained engagement with the analysis of international relations in ethical terms. They will have little sense of these authors taking on questions such as: What is a just war?, How should wars be fought?, When is humanitarian intervention justified? and so on. There may well be an ethical concern, but it is likely to be implicit rather than explicit. Overall, then, the professionals do not appear to hold much truck with our everyday concern and engagement with ethics in the international domain. Our everyday concern with such issues must then be taken to be naive, hypocritical or misguided.

TAKING THE ETHICAL TURN

This book takes issue with the position outlined above. It rejects the suggestion that the international domain is 'ethics-lite'. In what follows I attempt to show that the paradoxical position we find ourselves in arises from our having accepted a rather shallow understanding of the role of ethics in international affairs. These apparent paradoxes are dispelled if we advance to a more thorough grasp of the role of ethics in world affairs. In what follows I shall endeavour to make the case that, in order to participate in international relations, whether directly or relatively indirectly as an analyst, one cannot but be concerned with ethics at every point. What the argument will show is that hypocrisy is not to be found in those who purport to be concerned with the ethical dimensions of international interactions but quite the other way around; the hypocrites are those who purport simply to be interested in the imperatives of power politics. Their hypocrisy resides in the ways in which they conceal the fundamental ethical commitments which guide their actions both in theory-building and in policy-making.

Contrary to the commonplace assumptions discussed above, which suggest that international relations are best understood in

[margin note: Those who dismiss ethics are guilty of hypocrisy.]

advance certain privileged interests. Using theory is a mode of deploying power. See Ashley 1987, p. 409. Post-structural theorists also focus on changing technologies of power and how these become embodied in forms of knowledge such as 'governmentality' that now stretch beyond the boundaries of states. See Jabri 2007.

power-political terms, I shall argue that ethical concerns are central to our participation in international interaction at every point. I shall make this case by presenting a way of understanding contemporary international relations which, instead of portraying the field as occupied by actors such as states and individuals, understood as entities that are primarily concerned with advancing their interests in a world of ongoing power struggles, I shall argue that the key actors, both states and individuals, are best understood as entities that are constituted as actors of a certain kind within specific global social practices each with its own internal ethical structure (constitution). I shall show how these constitutive practices are themselves underpinned by rather thick sets of ethical values which constrain in severe and complex ways the actions of the actors thus constituted. In these social practices, actors must always be (and, indeed, always are) concerned to maintain their ethically constituted status. Where they fail to maintain this, it results in the actors' loss of standing in the practice concerned. In order to maintain their status actors have to demonstrate in what they do and say that they are upholding the ethics internal to their constituting international practices. What emerges from this form of analysis is that an engagement with ethics is not an option for participants but is a precondition of their participation. This form of analysis shows ethics to be centre stage for all international actors, including that class of actors we know as 'scholar/experts' in the field.

I need to pause briefly to accentuate the claim that I am making here. On the argument to be offered below, to engage in international relations at all (and everyone of us does so in any number of different ways) is to make ethical claims for oneself and to recognize the ethical standing of others. This includes that form of engagement we know as the scholarly analysis of international affairs. To put forward an analysis is to do something that may be judged right or wrong from an ethical point of view. To get one's analysis of an international interaction wrong is, amongst other things, to be guilty of an ethical wrongdoing. This proposition, of course, applies to the analysis being given here, too.

How am I to make this case about the centrality of ethics to everything we do in international affairs? By what means can I demonstrate that, in participating in international relations, we, together with all the other participants, need to be understood as actors fundamentally concerned about how our actions are being ethically appraised and as being fundamentally concerned with the ethical appraisal of the actions of others?

I shall do this by presenting a practice-based theory of international action. In terms of this theory we have to understand that international actors are constituted as such within global social practices which are underpinned by specific sets of ethical commitments. These constrain in a fundamental way what the actors thus constituted may do. Failure to abide by these constraints undermines the standing of the actors and, at the limit, results in their being excluded from these practices. Let me start then with a discussion of the relationship between actors, actions, practices and ethics.

SOCIAL PRACTICES, ACTORS AND ETHICS

The following analysis turns on the claim that to be an actor is to be a *participant* in a social practice. Thus, to be an international actor is to be a participant in a global practice. Crucially, being a participant in a social practice necessarily involves making evaluations about what, from an ethical point of view, it would be appropriate to do next. The analysis that follows turns on a particular understanding of the relationship between action, participation, social practices and ethics. This understanding is a general one and is applicable across all social forms from micro ones, such as families, meso ones, such as multinational corporations and beyond these to macro ones, such as global civil society and the system of sovereign states.

A participant in a social practice is an actor who, together with the other actors in the practice, acknowledges a complex set of rules which specify, amongst other things:

- who is qualified to be a participant
- what would count as disqualifying behaviour by a participant that would result in his/her exclusion from the practice
- what range of actions are available to qualified participants
- what actions are specifically disallowed to participants within the practice
- what procedures are appropriate for changing the rules of the practice
- what is to be done to those who flout the rules

- how to make an ethical evaluation of the history of interaction between the participants.

Crucially, for my present purposes, the participants in a social practice know what the ethical underpinnings of the practice are – these specify what the point and purpose of the practice are and what values are made possible within it. The ethical underpinnings specify what values are so fundamental to the participants in the practice that the flouting of these rules would result in the exclusion (excommunication, expulsion, ostracization) of actors who flout them.[23] Usually these fundamental ethical commitments are valued forms of mutual recognition that can only be had through participation in the practice in question.[24]

A quick example can demonstrate the core features of social practices mentioned above. International diplomacy is a social practice. In order to be recognized as a participant in it, one has to meet certain criteria and go through rigorous processes of recognition. Meeting these conditions is a requirement that has to be fulfilled before one can participate as a diplomat. Diplomats have a range of widely understood actions open to them, such as presenting their credentials and executing *démarches*. They know what conduct is disallowed within the practice. An example of what is not allowed is spying. Underlying the complex of rules that constitute the practice is a sophisticated set of ethical values, to do with promoting the well-being of the system of states through avenues of clear communication and so on.[25] It is crucial for participants in this practice to know how to evaluate from an ethical point of view the history of interactions within the system leading up to the current period. Such an historical account will make ethical judgements about who did what,

23 Many practices create relationships between the participants which are of fundamental ethical value to them. For example, for many Roman Catholics being a member of the church is not a means to an end but is of value in itself. Excommunication would, for such people, be an ethical disaster.

24 In families the core value is the value we attach to being recognized as a member of the family; in universities it is the value we attach to being recognized as a practising academic; in states it is the value we attach to being recognized as a citizen; and so on.

25 For a traditional account of the diplomatic practice see Nicolson, 1961, Anderson, 1993.

to whom and why, in the run-up to the present. Such an account must necessarily specify who, in this historical process, was wronged and who was not. A diplomat who was not able to do this would not be able to participate in this practice.

Having introduced the essentials of practice theory, we now need to ask: How do we know of any group of people whether or not they are participants in a social practice? How are we to determine where one practice ends and another begins? How do we know whether the people in a group are engaged in a single practice or whether they are simultaneously participating in a number of different practices? Most importantly, how do we determine what ethic is embedded in any given practice?

In brief, we know that a social practice exists through noting the existence of a pattern of claims and counterclaims between a group of people – by noting what they say about their own actions and about the actions of others. The existence of a social practice is indicated where between the members of a group of people we notice, through what they do and say, that they acknowledge the pertinence of a common set of criteria for appraising one another's actions. For example, you as an observer might notice that I, as an academic, acknowledge in a number of different ways that my actions may properly be appraised by other academics in terms of a set of criteria commonly recognized amongst us. You might find that my colleagues and I recognize rules pertaining to research practices, the use of sources, the testing of findings and the publication of the results of my research. It is our common recognition of the 'rules of the academic game' that identifies us to you as participants in the practice of academic life. My adherence to these determines my standing within the practice. That I am a participant is indicated by the vulnerability I display towards criticisms from my fellow participants in terms of these settled norms of academic life. The set of criteria binding participants in this (and other) social practices has a more or less clear border. The border is indicated by those criticisms of others to which we pay no attention – to the criticisms that we take as not being relevant to us. For example, my status as an academic is not at all vulnerable, to put it glibly, to the criticisms of 'flat earthers', members of cults based on superstition and so on. Similarly, participants in the practice of chess are vulnerable to the criticisms of fellow chess players who acknowledge a core set of settled norms of chess, but they are not vulnerable to those who might criticize them from the point of view of some other game. A final example is provided by the participants in the global market. They are vulnerable in what they do and say, to the criticisms of fellow participants in the market – to those who appraise their actions in terms of a key set of settled norms. They are not vulnerable to evaluations offered by communists and others who reject markets, *tout court*.

In summary, then, a practice exists where we find people offering to one another explanations and justifications for what they do by referring to a commonly accepted set of 'rules of the game'.[26] As already indicated, this feature of social practices, the vulnerability of participants to the criticism of other participants, implies the existence between them of mutually recognized maxims, rules and norms in terms of which they make their justifications and criticisms. These need not be rules or norms that are overtly articulated. They may simply be tacitly understood. Participants show their understanding of such rules by knowing what counts as getting a particular action right and what would count as having made a mistake in the execution of the action. In order to become a participant in a practice a person has to learn what the constitutive rules, norms and maxims of the practice are, for these determine who is to count as a legitimate participant and what is to count as appropriate conduct within the practice. Appropriate conduct in turn determines one's standing as an actor in the practice in question.

It is central for the purposes of this book that we take note of the following insight of practice theory. When seeking to understand a practice it is important to ascertain from what people say about it (whether it be a family, a church, a sport or a corporation) what the underlying ethic of that practice is. For in all practices the participants hold to some underlying ethic which justifies the 'rules of the game' seen in the round. *It is this internal ethic which enables them to make sense of what they do within the practice.* In what follows I shall use the following phrases interchangeably to refer to the internal ethic of social practices: internal ethic, background ethical theory, ethical foundation and ethical basis.

The relationships between participants within any social practice are quite different to those which obtain between actors who are not

26 We might also refer to these as 'settled norms'.

participating in such a common practice. A hypothetical example can illustrate this point. Consider the relationships that might hold between the members of an expeditionary force to a foreign place and the people they might encounter there. Suppose they stumble across a gathering of such 'foreigners', but do not know what they are doing. They find that they do not know how to respond to what may, or may not be, criticisms from these people. This would be a clear case where we would say that there was no social practice incorporating both the members of the expeditionary group and the foreigners. We would have to say that the two groups were simply *encountering* one another, rather than *participating* (or *interacting*) in a common social practice. In such an encounter the people from both groups would no doubt experience incomprehension, bewilderment and confusion. They would be akin to explorers encountering a foreign tribe in the way that the Spaniards encountered the Aztecs and the Incas when they first arrived in South America. A central theme of this book, then, is that contemporary international relations are not properly understood if they are understood as a set of encounters. They are better understood as a set of interactions. This requires practice theory.

All of us are normally simultaneously participants in a large number of social practices, such as families, churches, schools, universities, political parties, corporations and states, to mention but a few. The relationship between these multiple practices is complex, subject to ongoing change and often contentious. Participation in some of them is a prerequisite for participation in others. In some cases the opposite is true, participating in one practice rules out the possibility of bona fide participation in others.[27] Over time, some practices may have formed the foundation for subsequent more sophisticated practices.[28] For the moment, I have said enough to indicate in a general way what a social practice is and how one might go about determining that one exists. I have also indicated how participation requires knowledge of and adherence to the background ethic embedded in it.

---

27 Ongoing membership of the Roman Catholic Church precludes any possibility of a person converting to Judaism and vice versa.

28 For example, participation in the practice of reading is a prerequisite for entry into to the practice of university life.

Let us now return to our specific focus, international relations. Are there any international practices that involve most people in most places? By paying attention to the claims and counterclaims that we make upon one another in the global context, it is abundantly clear that there are at least two international practices. The one we might call global civil society (GCS) and the other the society of sovereign states (SOSS). Their existence is indicated by the fact that for each we acknowledge a body of settled rules, norms and maxims, which together establish who is to count as a participant, what array of permissible actions are available to participants, what actions are prohibited, what countermeasures are appropriate in the face of transgressions, how new rules may come into being and so on. Worldwide we find actors using these settled norms to grant one another valued standing as actors of a certain kind, to act in certain permitted ways, to justify their actions in well-known terms, to criticize wrong action on the part of other actors and to defend their own actions in the light of the criticism of others. The participants in this practice (that is, us) also, in some measure, know and understand the values that implicitly underpin the total set of settled norms. They criticize those who seek to undermine these. They show themselves to be vulnerable to such criticism coming from other actors in the practice.

Crucially, in these, as in other practices, participants (those who have been constituted as actors in them) must always be concerned about the 'fit' of their actions with the underlying ethic of that practice. As participants they have to scan the conduct of others and their own past and future conduct in order to determine whether or not their actions are appropriate to the underlying ethic embedded in these practices.

In the normal course of events securing the fit is easy and straightforward. In everyday international conduct the fit between action and the underlying ethic is present in an uncontentious way. Thus, in the system of sovereign states, for example, when two or more states sign a free trade agreement (such as NAFTA) the participants understand that doing this kind of thing fits with the ethical values embedded in the inter-state practice within which they are participating. This is the kind of thing that states are authorized to do within the practice of sovereign states. This is ethically justifiable conduct. Similarly, when individual rights holders buy and sell products to one another in the global practice of civil society, the actors recognize that this is the kind of thing authorized by the ethic underlying the practice, although there are well-known limits on the class of things it is ethically appropriate to buy and sell. Selling people is outside this limit. Similarly, members of international practices know the range of actions that are ethically inappropriate to these practices. For example, when the officers of a state squirrel away public money into private bank accounts, there is widespread recognition by the other participants that this conduct is inappropriate in terms of the basic ethic of the practice of states. The miscreants know this, too, and go to lengths to conceal their deeds, for they well understand the public criticism that would come their way if their deeds became publicly known.

To repeat the central point, understanding what is deemed ethically appropriate conduct is a prerequisite for participation in social practices, including our international ones. Those who do not understand the embedded ethic risk acting inappropriately and thus risk exclusion, ridicule, punishment and often laughter from the other participants. To use an extreme example, even the rumours that Idi Amin 'President for Life' in Uganda and 'Emperor' Bokassa in the Central African Republic ignored the ethic embedded in the practice of sovereign states that eating one's fellow citizens is wrong resulted in their being internationally ostracized and ridiculed.

We have seen then that international actors are, simply by virtue of their status as actors in international practices, vulnerable to ethical criticism from their fellow participants. This vulnerability arises from the fact that the actors are constituted as such through the recognition accorded them by their fellow participants. The recognition is granted or withheld according to whether or not the actors uphold the fundamental ethic embedded in the international practices. This vulnerability to ethical appraisal by the other participants is not dependent on the actors' power. Superpowers are as vulnerable as small powers. The process of ethical appraisal is ongoing for all actors in social practices throughout the different phases of participation, which include: appraising the context of action, considering options, justifying the choice of option and the carrying out of decisions arrived at.

There is an alternative way of expressing what I have outlined above. We may say that the rules, maxims, principles and the background ethic which supports them, taken together, create the conditions of possibility (COP) for a range of different actions by a specific actor in a given situation. A state deciding on a foreign policy within the practice of sovereign states has a range of policy alternatives open to it within the ethical COP created by that practice. For example, Britain has the option of strengthening its ties with the EU or not, strengthening the 'special relationship' with the USA or not, or some combination of these. All of these options may well be within the COP set down by the ethical constraints within the practice of states. It is not the case that the ethic embedded in a social practice only authorizes a single action as ethically appropriate in a given context. I am not making the case for structural determinism. The ethic makes possible a range of actions and sets the limits of that range. The ethic, together with its associated laws, rules and principles, creates an area of freedom for actors.

I call the approach to the analysis of international relations that I am outlining here 'constitutive theory'.[29] It focuses attention on how the key actors in international relations are constituted as such through the mutual recognition they give one another in terms of a standard set of 'rules of the international game'. More specifically it focuses on the ethical background theory which justifies the whole set of rules which constitute the practice. Constitutive theory is a particularly important mode of analysis because it brings to light that actors within a given social practice (or set of social practices) are constituted not just as actors but as ethical actors subject to ethical conditionalities. Their standing as actors depends on their adherence to a given set of ethical preconditions. Consider a state that never honoured its treaty commitments and often breached the requirements of international diplomatic protocol. Such a state would no longer be deemed a sovereign state in good standing within the international community of states. It might be termed a *pariah* or a

---

29 I first developed constitutive theory in Frost 1986 a work in which I sought to apply some of the core insights taken from GWF Hegel's *Philosophy of Right,* but without relying on Hegel's metaphysics Hegel 1973. This was reworked and extended in Frost 1996. I produced a further elaboration of constitutive theory in Frost 2002.

rogue state.[30] Let me briefly reiterate what distinguishes constitutive theory from other forms of social theory. In the first place it is a *holist* form of analysis. It starts from the assumption that we cannot make sense of human action and interaction without paying close attention to the social practices within which these take place. In order to do this we need to have an *insider perspective*. We need to understand the criteria actors use in interpreting and criticizing their actions and those of others. This highlights the importance of *understanding* rather than mere observation. Part of what is involved in this is paying attention to the forms of *reciprocal recognition* that we encounter within social practices. These stipulate criteria that determine who is to count as a participant in good standing and what would count as adequate reason to expel a participant from a practice. It focuses, thus, on how through such modes of mutual recognition we constitute one another as actors of a certain kind. A further key feature of constitutive theory is its focus on individual actors who are simultaneously constituted in multiple social arrangements that relate to one another in interesting and complex ways. Taken together these practices form the social architecture within which we are constituted as who we are. As these social practices evolve and change tensions emerge within this architecture. Of particular interest are the ethical tensions that arise from time to time.

POWER, POLITICS AND ETHICS

In the preceding section I have made the point that in order to become a participant in a social practice we need to be constituted as an actor in good standing within the practice. This involves learning the rules governing action within that practice (we might call these colloquially 'the rules of the game' even though many social practices are not games) and learning the ethic that underlies them.[31]

---

30 Consider an example from football. Imagine a very talented player who consistently cheated and flouted the rules of the game. No matter how good a player he was, no matter how 'strong' he was as a player, he would cease to be recognized as a player in good standing within the practice of football. It is easy to think of similar examples from any social practice whatsoever.

31 An alternative metaphor here might be taken from the practice of sailing where one talks of 'learning the ropes'.

Within social practices actors always have a range of options open to them within the ethical conditionalities imposed on them.[32] The practice creates areas of freedom for the participants.

Within any, and all, social practices, including international ones, actors with differing skills, different temperaments, different aims and ambitions, will make different uses of the options available to them within them – we might say that they will make different uses of the freedoms they have within those practices. Some will use them to their own advantage and will accumulate social power through their astute actions. Others will make bad choices with negative consequences for their long-term well-being. Whatever the rules in a given social practice, they will benefit some actors with certain natural attributes more than others. For example, in the practice of states, states that are rich in natural resources may well be able to prosper in ways not open to states less well endowed. Similarly, states that are well governed may prosper in ways that poorly governed states do not. Actors may use their advantages to form alliances with other astute actors in their respective practices, thus accumulating social power which they might then use to advance their own interests. They will accumulate that form of power that comes from acting in concert. The ethical constraints within practices are not antipathetic towards the accumulation of power *per se*; they merely set ethical limits to how this might legitimately be done. The common perception, discussed in the opening section of this book, that the international domain is one characterized by the pursuit of power by states, need not be read as indicating that this is a field in which ethical constraints do not have a hold on actors. Quite the contrary, in terms of the present analysis, we might say that the actors that pursue power in international relations are actors who are socially constituted and are, as such, ethically constrained. As actors of a certain kind they are required to seek power subject to the ethical constraints embedded in the practice. So, sovereign states, within the practice of sovereign states, are free (ethically authorized) to make arrangements with one another in order to advance what they consider their interests to be. The states of Southern Africa, for example, have formed the Southern African Customs Union. Its

---

32 This is a defining feature of what is involved in being an actor at all. To act is to initiate a deed from within a range of possibilities.

success has afforded to it power and prestige not enjoyed by states in the region which are not members. Within SACU, of course, the member states are still subject to the ethical constraints operative in the practice as a whole.

It has been pointed out that those who seek to maximize their power in international affairs (and in other spheres) are constrained by ethical considerations embedded in the practice of international relations. It is, however, important to stress that this does not mean that the actors are not *able* to flout the constraints. The constraints are not physical laws which dictate what is possible in the way that laws of gravity dictate the behaviour of a falling apple. The constraints of a practice can be flouted, but doing this will undermine the recognition accorded the actor and will thus affect his/her/its ethical standing. Were a state within the SACU to fail to honour the terms of its agreement with the other states of SACU, this would undermine its standing as an international actor.

In like manner, within all social practices it is possible to use the menu of ethical options available to one to pursue *political* ends. There are many different definitions of 'politics', but for my present purposes let me define 'politics' as 'action within a practice directed towards changing the fundamental rules of association'. An example of politics would thus be efforts to change the voting procedures in the UN Security Council. Another example of politics would be found in the efforts in the UN directed towards improving the procedures for dealing with humanitarian crises. Most social practices provide for ways of conducting politics that do not flout the ethical conditions of possibility of the actors doing the politics. Thus, within the existing international practices, the UN provides a forum for conducting politics within the ethical constraints imposed by these practices. International law specifies a number of ways in which new international law may be made and old law changed. It is, of course, possible that in pursuing political goals actors may well infringe the ethical constraints imposed on them. Obviously, this will undermine their standing within the relevant practice. For example, the contemporary international order provides a set of conflict resolution techniques to be used by states involved in disputes about borders. States that seek to resolve the issue by immediate resort to force are flouting the ethic of the international practice of sovereign states. Such action will bring down on the offending state a spate of international condemnation, which may well lead to action against it, as happened in the first war against Iraq in 1991.

Without extending this discussion too much, let me say a little more about the relationship between actors, action and social power. All social power derives either from actors acting in concert with the deliberate aim of reaching certain goals (as has happened in Europe, for example, through the creation of military alliances such as NATO) or from the structural effects of people following certain social rules over time. Structural power becomes manifest, for example, in the ongoing functioning of an economic market – some get rich and some remain poor. Who ends up rich or poor does not simply depend on individual effort, but depends on the structural position of participants in the market place. Those who start with capital (including educational capital) are more likely to end up rich than those who start with none. Those who are rich often turn out to have considerable social power simply by virtue of their social position. There is a vast literature dealing with the niceties involved in the analysis of power.[33] While these are interesting for specialists, they are not crucial for my current purposes. What is important for the present argument is that we note that all analyses of social power can only be launched once we have understood the deed or deeds of actors who have standing, including ethical standing, in some or other social practice within which they are constituted as actors of a certain kind. Thus it is that the kind of power that comes from the concerted action of states in treaty-based organizations can only be put together by states who have standing as sovereign states within a system of sovereign states. Maintaining this standing, the standing of being a participating state, requires general adherence to the ethical constraints internal to the system of states. Of course, within social practices like the SOSS some states might, from time to time, seek to flout the rules and ethical constraints, but this is a risk that can only be done occasionally. Similarly, within an economic practice the structural effects come from actors reiterating again and again the actions they are entitled to undertake within the marketplace – of particular importance here, of course, are the acts of buying and selling. To be a participant (a buyer or seller) one has to be in good standing within the global

33 See for example Lukes 1974 for a powerful introduction to a complex subject.

market place. Cheating, although possible, can only be done from time to time.[34]

THE PRIMACY OF ETHICS

We have seen then that the primary goal of a participant in a social practice, *qua* participant, must be to maintain his/her/its standing as a participant in that practice. This is primarily an ethical goal. It is 'ethical' in that it involves the participants inter-subjectively valuing one another as actors of a certain kind through adherence to rule-governed patterns of reciprocal recognition. The maintenance of the standing thus created is a precondition for whatever else the actor may wish to achieve within that practice. Maintaining status as a participant requires that actors correctly appraise the ethical constraints applicable to their status and that they do not fall foul of these. Passing this ethical test is crucial, for to fail it, is to lose standing within the practice and, at the limit, to be excluded from it. Consider some simple illustrations of this: For those seeking to maintain their standing as arbitrators in processes of international arbitration it is crucial that in what they do they remain true to the ethic embedded in the arbitration practice. A special envoy of the UN in order to maintain his/her status must remain true to the ethical underpinnings of that office. Similarly, a diplomat seeking to negotiate a treaty must maintain his/her good standing in the practice of diplomacy.[35]

In international relations, as in other social practices, actors are vulnerable to ethical appraisal by their fellow participants on an ongoing basis and through all the phases of an action. What aspects of an actor's activities are open to criticism include: an actor's analysis of a situation, the explanation of how it came about, the choice of

---

34 Rule-breaking and cheating of all kinds is only open to a few participants in any social practice and then only every now and again. Rule-breaking is parasitic on most people, being rule-abiding most of the time.

35 Examples can be adduced from any social practice whatsoever. In order to achieve one's goals in sport one must maintain one's status as a player in good standing; in order to achieve one's goals in a religious practice one must maintain one's good standing as a Buddhist, Christian or Hindu; in academic practice one must not abuse the ethical codes of academic life (truth-seeking, the anti-plagiarism rule and so on).

policy options, the justification of the chosen option and the execution of that option. All these are open to ethical appraisal by the actor's co-participants. There is no way in which one can make oneself secure against such appraisal in some permanent physical sense. Practice theory requires of us that we adopt an ethics-based understanding of security. At the heart of the matter is this: What has to be maintained here is inter-subjective ethical approval. The approval sought has to be sought and maintained in the public domain of the practice in question (it cannot be secured in some private deal on the side). The most devastating manoeuvre that can be delivered against a co-participant in a social practice is to be de-constituted as a participant, to be expelled, excommunicated, ostracized, ousted and so on. This ethical de-constitution or decommissioning of an actor is achieved not by some feat of physical force but by making the case that the actor has fallen foul of one or more constitutive norms – by showing that the immanent ethic of the practice has been severely breached through the action in question.

Because the process of ethical appraisal is so fundamental to our participation in social practices it ought not to surprise us that a lot of conflict in the practices of international relations can be construed as argument (in a very broad sense of the term) directed at securing a positive ethical appraisal for the participants' actions. While the ethical dimensions of interaction are always present in international relations, ethical disputes come to the fore in abnormal situations that present the actors with what might be termed 'hard cases'.

Before looking at such cases more closely, it is important to note that most actions in our international practices are ethically uncontentious. Day in and day out people, either as individuals or as collective actors (states, churches, multinational corporations), participate in our international practices in any number of uncontentious ways. They trade, migrate, tour, make financial deals, communicate (mail, phone, email, fax), undertake international sporting tours, engage in study abroad programmes and so on.[36] In these

---

36 Similarly, in other social practices the normal run of actions is ethically uncontentious – in universities academics get on with teaching and research, football players play football and so on. When they do these things, they automatically, as a matter of course, follow the ethic embedded in the social institution within which they are participating.

mundane actions the participants are simply able to rely on and take for granted the ethical soundness of both their own actions and those of others. The ethical soundness of the transactions is taken for granted. No conscious thought about the ethical dimensions of what they are doing is required.[37] However, even in these everyday ethically contentious actions, it is crucial that the actors know what the ethical constraints are. In order to act in an ethically contentious way, they need to know what would count as a wrongdoing on their own part or on the part of others. This comfortable state of affairs, though, is ruptured in those 'hard cases' where disputes arise about what is ethically required in the circumstances. Such difficult cases often emerge where there is a political dispute, that is, where there is a dispute about a fundamental rule(s) in the practice in question. This happens, for example, when there is a dispute about whether to intervene in the domestic affairs of another state. This can be understood as a dispute about the fundamental non-intervention rule of the practice of states. It is a political dispute.[38] Here one might expect argument to ensue about the ethical appropriateness of an interventionist action. Here the very stuff of the political dispute is an ethical matter – what the politics are about are ethical disputes. This needs to be elucidated.

Here are some contemporary examples of the ways in which we have to, and indeed do, understand many contemporary international interactions in ethical terms. When President George W. Bush launched operation Enduring Freedom in Afghanistan he was not simply authorizing his military forces to attack the Taliban (although he was doing this). Beyond unleashing his forces, he was wanting his action to be understood as the conclusion of an ethical argument that started with a wrong that had been done to the USA by the Jihadi who had flown their planes into targets in the USA on

---

37 The reader is invited to consider all the many mundane actions with an international dimension that he or she has done today and to consider the ethical assumptions that undergirded them. Examples might include telephoning, buying things, touring, reading, surfing the web or selling one's labour. All of these are ethically constrained, but for the most part we adhere to the constraints as a matter of course, without a second's thought.

38 Recall the definition of politics discussed earlier where politics was defined as thought and action among participants about the fundamental rules in terms of which they are associating.

9/11; this was backed up by other arguments that referred to a set of ethical values embodied in the constitution of the USA, to the values built into international law, to standards that condemn the use of terror as a means of conflict which in turn highlighted the ways in which the use of such means wrongfully harms innocent people, and so on. The military action by the coalition of the willing was framed in such a way that it was not merely to be understood as a deployment of force but was to be seen as a forceful action that the actors (the USA and its allies) wished to have interpreted in a very specific ethical way.

Similarly, the hijackers on 9/11, the Mujahidin and all the fellow travellers that sympathized with them did not want what they did to be interpreted merely as the deployment of force against the USA and its allies. They did not simply launch manned missiles at their targets (although, of course, they did this), but they sought to have the deed carry a certain meaning to the international audience.[39] The actors wished this to be interpreted in a specific ethically charged way. The act was a statement that needed interpretation. A key component of the ethical justification put forward by Al Qaeda and other groups sympathetic to it was a religious one referring to the tenets of Islam. These certainly carried no conviction for people not of the Islamic faith. However, parallel to this justification were a number of other arguments that have found resonance with many people worldwide. These referred to alleged injustices perpetrated against Muslims by despotic regimes, several of which have been supported by the USA and its allies. They also referred to the use of double standards by the USA and its allies in many parts of the world. The allegations of 'double standards' referred to the way in which notionally the USA and others stood for the promotion of democracy and the protection of human rights, but in many cases these values were not upheld, particularly in those cases where they were overridden by material interests.[40] There were also arguments about the injustice of the USA's uncritical support for the policies of Israel against the Palestinians and so on.

Here is a further example of what I mean when I claim that in

39 On the need to interpret international affairs in terms of meaning see Laidi, 1998.
40 For a discussion of some of these see Devji, 2005.

such hard cases international action is best understood as 'ethical argument broadly construed?' In a *New York Times* article headed 'The Long-Term Battle: Defining "Victory" Before the World', Steven Erlanger states

> As Israeli troops press the ground offensive in southern Lebanon, Israel is fighting now to win the battle of perceptions.[41]

In the meat of the article he makes the case that the Israeli government and those who support it internally and externally are taking great pains to present what they are doing in one ethical way rather than another. The case that they wish to make is that the ground offensive is not to be understood as an act of aggression against Lebanon or against the Palestinian people in Lebanon generally. Rather they wish to present it as an ethically justified act of self-defence against the movement Hezbollah. The opponents of Israel are, of course, seeking to push exactly the counterargument. They argue that what Israel is doing is ethically unjustified because it is an act of aggression, using disproportionate force against innocent people. The dispute here is not about the gloss to be put on an action, it is about the nature of the act itself.

A large component then of the conflictual activity in international relations consists in an ongoing struggle to promote one kind of ethical account (interpretation) of one's actions and policies rather than another. This is not something unusual in international affairs, nor is it something added on, as an afterthought, to the normal aims of actors in the field. For participants in the international practices of our time this struggle is always important. As indicated above, sometimes in everyday matters an actor knows that his own ethical standing and the status of his actions is uncontentious both for himself and for the others with whom he is interacting. In such cases the actor does not have to be concerned about how he himself or his deeds are being ethically appraised. He simply knows himself to be on ethically firm ground. The more difficult cases such as those discussed above are not like this at all. In these, the ethical case has to be made. These are the hard cases.

All actors in international affairs seek to have their actions interpreted in ethical terms. Israel has to make the case in its words and deeds that what it is doing is ethically acceptable to the international audience. If it fails in this, this will have severe consequences internationally. If it fails, there will be widespread international condemnation of what it has done. In the eyes of other states it will move towards pariah status. This condemnation is not merely rhetorical but will have consequences for its social, political, economic and military position in the world.[42] The government of a state not only has to present what it is doing as ethical to the international audience but it has to make the ethical case to its own domestic audience too.

For a further example of how fundamental ethical concerns are in our international interactions, consider the dispute between the Russian government and the Chechen nationalist movement which has played itself out over the past decade and a half. Throughout what was often a bloody and cruel conflict, various Chechen separatist groups sought to show up the Russian government's policies and actions towards Chechens as oppressive, as abusive of human rights, as denying to the Chechens their right to self-determination and as a form of state-backed terrorism. In the first Chechen War many Russian soldiers (including high-ranking officers) disputed the rightness of using excessive force against people who were Russian citizens. For a time there was some sympathy in Russia and abroad for the claims of the Chechens. But their claims encountered a rival set of claims. The Russian government claimed that the Chechen separatist groups were terrorists, that they abused human rights, that they sought to undermine the legitimate sovereign authority of the Russian state. Both sides in this dispute directed their arguments to both their domestic audiences and to the international audience. There are several things we need to notice in this and other such cases. The dispute – the argument – was not merely a verbal one, although, of course, it was that. Neither was it merely a physical one of force against force. The verbal propositions put forward to the domestic and international audience by all parties were closely tied

---

42 Such consequences became manifest when South Africa, Chile, Rhodesia, Libya and others found themselves outcasts within the international community of states. The ethical appraisal had very real results for these states. See Geldenhuys, 1990.

case-making. [handwritten]

Actions, as well as words, are part of the ethical [handwritten margin note]

to the violent deeds committed. By moving beyond mere words, the actors sought to show that they were in earnest about the arguments they were advancing. The actions, even the violent ones, must be understood as part and parcel of the case being made.[43] In the sphere of ethics a failure to act on what one professed would be a ground for doubting the argument put forward. A government that presented the argument that Al Qaeda was a terrorist group but failed to take anti-terrorist action would be inviting the audience to doubt its overall position. It would be held guilty of merely paying lip service to an ethical position of anti-terrorism. Similarly, an actor that vocally defended a human rights-based position but did not follow through with acts appropriate to that position would not be taken seriously. As things currently stand President Putin has successfully sidelined the separatists whom he argues are radical fundamentalist terrorists who oppose the moderate form of Sufism followed by the Islamic majority in the area. It is not my goal to present the historical details of this conflict. The example is used simply to illustrate that even in one of the most brutal of recent civil wars the ethical dimension is crucial at every point. To understand what the participants say and do we need to have views on the following ethical questions: Who is the legitimate authority? Who is employing legitimate means to promote its goals? Who is the terrorist?

But this is exactly what happens! (or the part of bigger state) [handwritten margin note]

Consider yet another example: Where a state or group of states professes itself to be in favour of free markets and where it defends this position with reference to a number of well-known liberal arguments but does not follow up this profession of a commitment to liberal values with support for the current round of WTO negotiations but instead seeks to maintain tariffs that protect local interests (e.g. farming interests), then we would be inclined to say that its ethical defence of liberal values was a sham.

A final case that demonstrates the point being made concerns migrants who sought entry into Australia under the 1951 Refugee Convention. The refugees claimed that they faced persecution in Indonesia and that they sought protection of their rights in Australia. They rested their case on an international legal instrument to which Australia is a signatory. That legal instrument itself is based on

---

43 The turn to violence does not mark the end of the attempt to present an ethical case to the world, but must be understood as a different way of making the case.

strong ethical arguments indicating the flaws of tyranny and the good to be found in human rights protection. The asylum seekers did not merely make a verbal argument justifying their stance but their actions in taking to boats en route for Australia were guided by the argument. By boarding boats and fleeing to Australia they demonstrated to the international audience that what they were doing was congruent with what they professed. For its part the Australian government claimed that the claims made by these 'refugees' were bogus – that they presented themselves as threatened with rights abuse whereas they were in fact economic refugees. This rhetorical position then became embodied for a while in a series of policy measures which included diverting the boats with refugees to a number of Australian islands which, through executive *fiat*, had been excised from the migration zone of the Australian state.[44] Here once again, in the confrontation between the antagonists, both put to the international audience their verbal arguments backed and supported by their deeds. The audience, the total international community, was in effect asked to determine who had the best of the ethical argument? The excising of parts of Australia from its migration zone meant that asylum seekers who landed in these excised territories lost rights that they might previously have claimed. The laws meant that asylum seekers could not automatically apply for refugee status and enabled Australia to move them to third countries (such as Nauru) who were paid a fee for receiving them.

These examples are illustrations of the way in which international actors may be seen as active in an ongoing way in the process of ethical appraisal outlined in the previous sections. On the view that I have advanced here, these actions, understood as arguments broadly conceived, do not represent some 'thin' aspect of international relations but must be understood as fundamental to the actors in question. They are 'fundamental' in that they pertain to how the actors

44 'This excising of Australia's migration zone meant that asylum seekers who landed in these excised territories lost rights that they would otherwise have been entitled to. The laws meant that asylum seekers could not automatically apply for refugee status and enabled Australia to move them to a third country while their applications were processed' (De Tarczynski 2008).

are constituted in international practices.[45] It is through these broad arguments that the actors attempt to maintain their standing in the relevant international social practices. Our ethical engagement, one may say, has to be 'thick' or 'substantial' at every point.

In general, then, my argument is that we often fail properly to engage with all the ethical dimensions of our international relations.[46] We might have noticed the ubiquity of ethical terms used when we give accounts of what happens in international affairs and in accounts of what we have done, but we have failed to realize just how fundamental these ethical justifications are to our participation in this realm. Instead, we have tended to see the domain as one in which ethics plays a minor role which is overshadowed by those of politics and power. Our self-understandings of what it is we are doing when we participate in international relations has been faulty. Later I shall show how this failure has given rise to some mistaken interpretations of events in world politics. These in turn have lead to the adoption and pursuit of many ill-considered policies. Later I shall show how a particularly grievous example of this is to be found in many of the actions taken by a diverse range of actors with regard to the so-called 'global war on terror'. The morass of bewilderment and anguish into which this so called 'war' has plunged us has not come about because we have failed to identify the proper enemy, or because we have failed in intelligence gathering about the enemy, or because we have failed to deploy sufficient force, or because we lack political will, or because the 'enemy' is cleverer than we are but because we have failed to understand the phenomenon of international 'terror' in all its ethical complexity. This set of problems does not arise only for the so called 'West' but also besets the

45 The argument being offered here is one which opposes the view that states may be understood as autarkic actors who may or may not concede to being bound by a 'thin' set of ethical principles. On the view being presented here, to be a state is to occupy a status conferred by a social practice. Outside of the recognition conferred on a state by the other states in the practice a state-like entity is not a state. The people of Quebec might wish to form a state, but Quebec is not a state because it is not recognized as such within the practice of states. On the criteria for gaining recognition as a sovereign state see Brownlie, 1979.

46 I suggest that we would be less likely to do this were we to talk of 'international interactions' rather than 'international relations'.

'enemy', who are similarly subject to ethical misunderstandings and confusion.

As participants in international affairs we have been making a mistake in the way that we analyse what we do. The mistake, I have suggested, is that we have failed to understand just how international relations consist of an ongoing ethical engagement *within* a specific set of international social practices. We have failed to engage with sufficient sophistication with the *sittlichkeit* within which we are participating.

What would a good analysis look like? What difference would such an analysis make to our day-to-day participation in these practices? What changes would this approach recommend with regard to the discipline of IR? These are key questions in what follows.

UNDERSTANDING INTERNATIONAL RELATIONS IN ETHICAL TERMS

[handwritten margin note: and How one goes about deciding/ learning the rules of the game'.]

The analysis presented above has been abstract and formal. The insights offered by practice theory as outlined above apply generally to all actors across the whole range of social practices. This includes families, schools, churches, corporations, states and the interstate system. Although I have given illustrative examples taken from the international domain, I have so far said little about the specific form and structure of our global international practices and about the struggles for ethical standing that takes place within them. Let me now turn to the international sphere with a view to demonstrating how this form of analysis can throw light on what we do and have done in our inter- and intra-practice international life.

As we have seen above, practice theory claims that in order to understand individual actions these have to be located in the broader context of the practices within which the actors are socially constituted. According to constitutive theory we have to pay particular attention to the ethical underpinning of these. How might we go about doing this? How does one determine the shape, form and ethical underpinnings of a practice within which one is already a participant? By definition as a participant one already knows some of the 'rules of the game'. Knowing these is a precondition for participation by any 'player' in any social 'game'. In order to fill out the details a participant must start with his own understanding of the rules. This might be quite rudimentary. This understanding might then be supplemented by asking other participants for their understandings, referring to written rule books, asking learned commentators and so on. Another method might involve finding the rules by testing the limits of the practice. This might be done by trying out various courses of action in order to elicit praise and criticism from other participants. One might not agree with the criticisms offered by one's fellow participants and an argument about what is to count as a proper interpretation of the rules might then ensue. From such arguments a richer and more developed overall profile of the practice will emerge. Here is a hypothetical example about how such a testing procedure might work.

> Minister of Defence: Would it be appropriate for me to authorize the launch of drones from our state to maintain surveillance over suspected terrorists in a neighbouring state?
>
> International Lawyer responds: If this were done without the permission of the government of the neighbouring state, this would amount to illegal intrusion into the air space of a sovereign state.
>
> Minister of Defence: But the neighbouring state is harbouring terrorists, which is not permitted in international law. (Refers to UN's International Convention for the Suppression of Terrorist Bombings 1997) and other anti-terror conventions. This law is to prevent terrorists from undermining international law.
>
> International Lawyer: The task of controlling such terrorists falls to the government of the sovereign state in which they operate.
>
> Minister of Defence: When the government fails to do this then it is up to other states in the international community to intervene.

It is easy to see how such an argument would take the discussants into a thoroughgoing consideration of the core rules of the practice of states and a discussion of the ethical underpinnings of these rules. It is through such arguments that the complexities and limits of the practice may be explored. It is difficult to envisage an alternative procedure.

In order to do this in the international realm we have to undertake the following steps: First, we must examine the accounts that participants in the international domain give of their own conduct and the conduct of others. In these actions and reactions there are often competing accounts of what is being done. Our search must be for the most coherent of these. Second, we are to scrutinize their assessments for the terms that point towards the ethical criteria embedded in the constituting practices. Third, we need to construct an encapsulating ethical theory which enables us to make the best possible sense of the full set of ethical criteria identified in the previous step. Finally, we can then turn back to the original accounts given by the participants to see which of them best accords with the ethical theory thus constructed. This will enable us to determine who has fared well and who badly in the struggle for ethical standing in these international practices.

Central to every application of an ethics-centred approach to the analysis of international affairs is the identification of the global practices within which individual actors and actions are located. In the following sections I shall show how, through the close analysis of a single set of international interactions, we can construct a picture of the global practice, with its ethical foundations within which the interactions are taking place. This will then help us provide rich ethical interpretations of specific actions taking place in global politics. As an illustrative example of how this might be done, I shall discuss that set of international interactions we currently refer to as the war in Iraq.[47]

The first step then is to determine what the actors themselves say they are doing. Constitutive theory suggests that the actors engaged in the current war in Iraq, in order to give an account of their actions, have to attend to the following ethical dimensions of their engagement: the ethical history of the state of affairs they are confronting (or which they confronted in the past) – this includes the series of actions and reactions that gave rise to the war; the

---

47 No particular significance ought to be read into this choice of example; any example from the realm of international events would do. One could refer to the conflict between Ethiopia and Eritrea, the ongoing conflict in Darfur in the Sudan, the disputes surrounding the Doha Round of the WTO, the international developments surrounding the war in Afghanistan, issues to do with migrants into the EU and so on.

ethical self-understandings of the key actors at the end of this history; an ethical assessment of the policy choices available to the actors; an ethical assessment of the policies chosen; an evaluation of the means of execution of the policies chosen; and an evaluation of the outcomes brought about as a result of the policies chosen. When combined into a single narrative these form the actor's appraisal of what is happening.[48] Of course, different actors might produce different appraisals of the same set of actions. By paying attention to these we can put together a comprehensive account of the global arrangements within which these disputes take place. Let us look at a range of appraisals of the current war in Iraq to demonstrate how the theory might be applied.

One such appraisal of this war is the Baker Hamilton Report (BHR). This was produced by the Iraq Study Group, a bipartisan commission set up by Congress to take stock of the war and to recommend policy to the USA Administration. Let us consider this appraisal and then consider a range of rival assessments that were produced in reaction to it.

The Baker Hamilton Report (BHR) itself and the reactions to it are all interventions in the flow of activity that comprises the conflict. Interpreters of the conflict, although not themselves in the front line of the fighting, are nevertheless participants in the war. Through the production of their reports, the authors (and we who comment on them) are participating in the international practices within which the war is taking place. As indicated earlier, these acts of participation may be read as ethical arguments broadly conceived aimed at convincing our fellow participants of the ethical merits of the cases being made. In interpreting the reports that I set out below, we ourselves have to assess the ethical merits of the case(s) being made. Let us now turn to this task.

---

48 In what follows I use the words 'appraisal', 'account', 'assessment' and 'evaluation' interchangeably. In using these terms I follow customary usage according to which we use these terms to include elements of historical insight, contemporary understanding, social explanation, empirical description and ethical evaluation. When calling for an assessment of a situation one is calling for verbal statements that include elements of all of these. There is also a built-in assumption that the assessment should be as concise as possible.

WAR IN IRAQ UNDERSTOOD IN ETHICAL TERMS: THE BAKER HAMILTON REPORT AND OTHER INTERPRETATIONS

Let us attend closely to a portion of the executive summary of the BHR:[49]

The situation in Iraq is grave and deteriorating. There is no path that can guarantee success, but the prospects can be improved. In this report, we make a number of recommendations for actions to be taken in Iraq, the United States, and the region. Our most important recommendations call for new and enhanced diplomatic and political efforts in Iraq and the region, and a change in the primary mission of U.S. forces in Iraq that will enable the United States to begin to move its combat forces out of Iraq responsibly. We believe that these two recommendations are equally important and reinforce one another. If they are effectively implemented, and if the Iraqi government moves forward with national reconciliation, Iraqis will have an opportunity for a better future, terrorism will be dealt a blow, stability will be enhanced in an important part of the world, and America's credibility, interests, and values will be protected. The challenges in Iraq are complex. Violence is increasing in scope and lethality. It is fed by a Sunni Arab insurgency, Shiite militias and death squads, Al Qaeda, and widespread criminality. Sectarian conflict is the principal challenge to stability. The Iraqi people have a democratically elected government, yet it is not adequately advancing national reconciliation, providing basic security, or delivering essential services. Pessimism is pervasive. If the situation continues to deteriorate, the consequences could be severe. A slide toward chaos could trigger the collapse of Iraq's government and a humanitarian catastrophe. Neighbouring countries could intervene. Sunni-Shia clashes could spread. Al Qaeda could win a propaganda victory and expand its base of operations. The global standing of the United States could be diminished. Americans could become more polarized. During the past nine months we have considered a full range of approaches for moving forward. All have flaws. Our recommended course has shortcomings, but we firmly believe that it includes the best strategies and tactics to positively influence the outcome in Iraq and the region.

49 Baker, Hamilton & and others, 2006, pp. 6–8.

In this paragraph an assessment of the overall state of affairs is made and some policy recommendations are put forward. The ethical content of the assessment is to be found in the assertion that there is a democratically elected government facing violence emanating from, amongst other things, a 'Sunni Arab insurgency, Shiite militias and death squads, Al Qaeda, and widespread criminality. Sectarian conflict is the principal challenge to stability . . .'. Here the Iraqi government is framed as the ethically good actor. But, even though its ethical credentials are better than those of its adversaries, it is to be criticized for failing in its attempts at 'advancing national reconciliation, providing basic security, or delivering essential services'. Notice that these are ethical criticisms. These are to be read as the good things, ethically speaking, that the government ought to be doing. The goal for the US, the report says, ought to be to withdraw its troops responsibly and to give the Iraqi government an opportunity to achieve national reconciliation and establish a better future. These, too, are ethical goals. Beyond this the ethical goal of the USA is to strike a blow against terrorism, which is taken to be ethically noxious, to ensure stability and to bring it about that 'America's credibility, interests, and values will be protected'. A failure might result in governmental collapse in Iraq, a humanitarian disaster, intra-Islamic conflict, a victory for Al Qaeda and a loss of international standing for the USA. A central thing for us to notice here is that a failure to achieve these goals would result in the US's loss of moral standing. The USA, instead of being seen as the promoter of good things such as human rights and democracy, would be seen by the international community as the state that caused the collapse of a government and thus precipitated a humanitarian disaster.

Before moving on, let me repeat that this assessment creates, and is intended to create, a detailed ethical picture for us, the audience, who read it. Crudely put, the USA is presented as the 'good guy' trying to promote a democratically elected government facing the 'bad guys' who are the insurgents, militias, death squads, Al Qaeda and criminals. It can only do this by assuming that we, the audience for this report, are fellow participants in a common practice of ethical commitments.

The Baker Hamilton appraisal is, of course, not the only possible account of the situation prevailing at the time. Compare the assessment and recommendations of the BHR with a rival assessment, with that provided by another participant in the war – this time one from the press. Matthew Parris in *The Times,* under the heading 'I should welcome the Baker Report, so why do I feel sick?' (Parris, 2006), appraises the report and a fortiori the situation in Iraq as follows:

It is shallow and dishonest. It shows how to weasel a way out of trouble and leave former friends to fall, undefended, by the wayside. It suggests how blame may be shifted onto hapless Iraqi ministers, and fatuous 'milestones' and 'timetables' confected with a view to their being demonstrably missed. It explains how international conferences may be set up in order that they should fail. For Britain and the United States, Baker is now, with no shadow of doubt, the only way out. So is 'Forward with James Baker III!' to be my banner?

Well it should be. But something rises in my gorge at the moral and intellectual shabbiness of the exercise. If we have lost this war, and with it the likely capacity to forestall the vacuum that our defeat will surely leave behind, shouldn't we just say so?

Only once do Baker and Hamilton engage with the cruelest question. They answer it quickly, flatly – and move on. 'If,' they say, 'the Iraqi Government does not make substantial progress toward the achievement of milestones on national reconciliation, security, and governance, the United States should reduce its political, military, or economic support for the Iraqi Government.' . . . the ISG report is really about a timetable for American withdrawal. The withdrawal is finally unconditional. Baker says so . . .

Notice, not only in James Baker's but also in Tony Blair's and George W. Bush's remarks, a newly reproachful tenor in bewailing the Iraqi administration's 'failure to take control' of militias or 'root out corruption' in the police. As though it could. As though the thought simply hadn't occurred in Baghdad that this might be a good idea. As though that al-Maliki fellow just needs boxing about the ears to get up off his backside, reconcile his warring countrymen, find out who those shockingly corrupt policemen are and sack them – and then sort out the security situation. Goodness me – we never thought of that!

I do find this odious. Those in the Government in Baghdad are at their wits' end and sinking: powerless to defeat what they hardly need Baker to tell them are the causes of the disaster unwinding on their doorsteps. They and their problems are the creation of British and

American policy and if Mr al-Maliki's Government cannot achieve what Britain and America want in Iraq, it ill-behoves us to establish (in Baker's phrase) 'milestones' for him to reach, to rail at him when he fails to reach them, and then to walk out in disgust at the lack of progress – as though only the Iraqi administration's foolish shortcomings had cheated the Forces of Freedom of victory . . .

In this column we are given an assessment of the ethical argument that was presented to us in the BHR. Parris suggests that the report paves the way for withdrawal, wrongly portrays the powers in the region as wanting peace, puts the blame for the instability on the government of Iraq and in no way makes mention of the USA and British role in causing this state of affairs. Throughout, there are a host of words used that in this context have an ethical dimension, including 'weasle', 'friends', 'fatuous', 'moral and intellectual shabbiness', 'blame', 'confected', 'set up to fail' and 'cynicism'.

The short version of the ethical argument presented by Parris is that the BHR seeks to set up the Iraqi government as being the party to blame for both the present set of problems and for what transpires after the USA withdrawal. A failure is anticipated and the ground is being laid for the apportioning of blame in the future. This is morally noxious, he says, because the civil war that pertains at the moment is largely the fault of the USA invasion in the first place.

Let us look at a third assessment of the same set of circumstances. After the production of the BHR and in the light of that report, the Administration of President George W. Bush drew up a new policy governing its engagement in Iraq. In some measure it accepted recommendations from BHR, but in other places it rejected them. The new Bush assessment, while accepting the needs for political and diplomatic efforts, still posited a role for a final military push in specified areas. It posited a need for what it called 'a surge' in forces prior to withdrawal. But it, too, cast the blame for the current civil war on insurgents and criminals. While not blaming the Maliki government, in power at the time, there were clear warnings to it that if it did not perform the USA would cease supporting it.[50]

In its assessment of the same state of affairs, the Iraqi government

50 President Bush, 'The new way forward in Iraq'; http://www.whitehouse.gov/news/releases/2007/01/20070110–3.htm.

rejected the report for wrongly blaming it for the dire circumstances that pertained at the time. It refused to accept this blame.

A fifth assessment of the same set of events is to be found in the press sympathetic to Al Qaeda. It portrayed the situation in a different light, stressing that the USA must be seen as an occupying force in a sovereign state. It portrayed the USA and its allies as advancing a crusade against Islamic people both through its involvement in Iraq but also through their ongoing support of Israel.

In a sixth assessment the government of Iran advanced a different assessment of the BHR, saying that it was happy to become involved in a regional initiative to stabilize the situation. However, it indicated that it was only willing to do this if the USA was prepared to meet with it to have a serious discussion about the region as a whole. In an article in *Time Magazine* it was reported that

> The Iranian Foreign Minister Manouchehr Mottaki dangled an offer of cooperation in a statement published by an Iranian news agency. "Iran will support any policies returning *security, stability and territorial integrity* to Iraq," he said, "and considers withdrawal of U.S. forces from Iraq and leaving security to the Iraqi government as the most suitable option." In an interview on Al Jazeera, Mottaki added that if the U.S. needs an "honourable way out of Iraq," Iran "is in a position to help" (*Time Magazine*, 2006).

Here the Iranian Foreign Minister is portraying his country as being in a position to be a force for good (promoting security, stability and territorial integrity to Iraq) and offering the USA an honourable way out of its dilemma in Iraq – the suggestion being, of course, that dishonour is staring the USA in the face. Contrast this with the way in which Iran was portrayed in the BHR where it was said to be actively encouraging the instability in Iraq by supporting Shiite insurgents. In the Iranian assessment, again, as always, the appraisal is shot through with ethical judgements.

The first thing to note about all these appraisals about what was happening in Iraq, together with their suggestions about what ought to be done, is that they were not all agreed on a neutral description of the state of affairs that existed at the time. They did not all agree on some objectively determinable set of facts which 'existed on the ground' to which they each then added their own prescriptive element. Instead, each presents us with a 'description' of the state of affairs that is, one might say, 'ethically drenched' from the outset. Instead of calling them 'descriptions' it is more accurate to say that what were presented to us, the international audience, were different appraisals, accounts, assessments or evaluations of the situation. A fundamental constituent of all of them was the ethical dimension.[51] The appraisals we have looked at are shot through and through with ethical judgements about who is to blame for the current state of affairs, about whose moral burden it is to rectify them and about what would be ethically appropriate policies given the circumstances. In the face of these rival and conflicting appraisals, a key question now becomes: How are we to appraise these appraisals?

At this point a standard relativist response might be that we cannot appraise the appraisals. All we can do is note these different ethical 'takes' on the Iraqi conflict. We should take note of the different value slopes implicit in each of these analyses. There is no way to determine the 'right' one. The view that there is nothing more to be done arises from the idea that these value slopes are choices which the actors make – that they are subjective choices that are neither right nor wrong. These subjective choices are then used to frame the history, present conduct and future options of the key actors involved. On this account there can be no appraisal of the appraisals because this itself would simply be another subjective choice, another subjective appraisal.

In contrast to this view, the argument of this book is that, because these assessments are all made from *within* existing international social practices, no assessor is entitled to unilaterally define what the correct assessment of the situation should be. Because the practices themselves are inter-subjective realities, this gives us a vantage point from which we can evaluate and argue about rival assessments. Each one may be examined to determine the extent to which it coheres (or fails to cohere) with the ethicality that is embedded in the relevant global practice. In short, the individual assessments are open to public criticism within the social practice within which they are located.

Which of these assessments best meshes with the values implicit in the international practices within which these assessors are

---

51 The point can be even more strongly stated thus: No account of the situation in Iraq can be given which is ethically neutral.

constituted as international actors? We can only answer this once we have identified the relevant practices and have determined what their ethical underpinnings are.

To repeat this point which is at the very heart of the present argument: The rival assessments set out above are all offered by international actors constituted as such within the same global practices. The assessors are co-participants in these global practices. As such they are directing their evaluations at their fellow participants in these practices. At every point these assessors are engaged in an argument with one another. In this engagement they are constrained in the appraisals they are entitled to make by the ethical commitments embedded in the constituting practices. That they themselves are constituted as actors within these global practices gives us a vantage point from which we can evaluate their respective appraisals.[52]

What then is, or are, the relevant global social practice(s) from within which we can evaluate these rival appraisers? Following from our earlier analysis of practices we know that the route to determining the existence of a practice and the identities of the participants in it is through an examination of the language that people use. Where there is a reciprocal vulnerability to criticisms in terms of certain sets of criteria, this indicates participation in a common practice. The criticisms identify who is to count as a legitimate actor, what menu of ethically appropriate actions are available to such actors and what list of actions are considered out of bounds and so on. The language reveals the self-understandings of the actors and these self-understandings reveal the parameters of the practice(s) within which they are constituted as actors.

---

52 It is important to note here that I am not simply making the case that the appraisers under consideration (the authors of the BHR, Matthew Parris, the Iraqi government, the Iranian government and the press sympathetic to Al Qaeda) are all constituted as actors in different social practices. Making this case would not give us any vantage point from which to evaluate the different appraisals. Instead, what I am claiming is that all the appraisers are participants in one or more *common* global practices. This opens the way for us to evaluate their appraisals in terms of a common ethicality. If they were not engaged in any common practices there could be no argument – there could be no assessment of their assessments. Instead, what transpired between them would have to be seen as a series of encounters that would be incomprehensible to the different parties.

The language use indicates who are to be taken as the legitimate actors in this 'war'. The language shows us, not surprisingly, that the actors whose conduct is being appraised are sovereign states within the society of sovereign states.[53] The actors making the appraisals are themselves participants, as citizens of sovereign states, in the practice of states. The assessments offered all draw on criteria which identify states (and the citizens in them) as legitimate actors. They all draw on criteria which specify what is to count as good conduct by citizens and states *vis-à-vis* one another. Some of the assessments drawing on these criteria point to insurgents, militias, Al Qaeda, death squads and criminals as people who have fallen foul of these criteria. They indicate that these actors have been disqualified from participation in this sphere of activity. Yet many of these 'wrongdoers' themselves rely on arguments which suggest that they, too, regard sovereign states as legitimate entities that are entitled to be autonomous and free of foreign occupation. They offer criticisms of specific actions of states such as the USA, Israel, Britain, Jordan and others that have fought in the coalition, but these criticisms indicate an assumption that normally sovereign states are legitimate and that the system of sovereign states itself is ethically sound. The argument is that in this specific case these states have behaved contrary to the appropriate norms.[54]

In the assessments we have also been given ethical evaluations of actions undertaken and actions proposed. The BHR identifies the actions of the insurgents et al. as perpetrating violence, which is clearly to be understood as ethically unacceptable. It calls for the use of ethically acceptable force by the democratically elected Iraqi government against the insurgents. This is to be understood as police work which would make use of the legitimate deployment of

---

53 I say 'not surprisingly' because we are all participants in this practice and, as such, we recognize from the 'internal point of view' the practice that informs their analysis. We are not investigating a strange or foreign practice. We are not like anthropologists investigating the practices of a foreign tribe.

54 In his speeches Osama Bin Laden repeatedly makes reference to the USA as an 'occupier' and a 'crusader'. This is easily read as referring to the non-intervention norm in the practice of states. He says that there will be no peace until such time as the USA troops go home. Here again legitimacy is accorded to the boundary-maintenance commitments of the society of states. See his speeches on 2 July 2006 and 8 September 2006. Translations available at (Bin Laden, 2007).

violence. It recommends that the USA shift its military mission from overt military action to the training of the enforcement branches of the Iraqi government. This training is to be understood as being ethically acceptable.

In contrast, the Parris article offers a different ethical evaluation of past and proposed actions by the sovereign states involved. Where the BHR puts the blame on the Iraqi government for its failure to curb the violence by the insurgents and other groups, Parris admits that the Iraqi government has failed in this, but lays the blame for this failure on the USA and its coalition allies for causing the disastrous current situation in the first place. The newly formed government cannot be blamed for failing to control a set of circumstances not of its making. He also recommends that the USA leave, but thinks that failure by the Iraqi government is inevitable. He calls for an apology from the USA and the UK for having caused this carnage. They should simply accept their loss of face and standing in this set of interactions.

The assessment of the Iranian government accepts that the key players with ethical legitimacy are the governments of the states involved. The Foreign Minister's estimation is that an ethically acceptable outcome can be achieved, but that it will require the USA to give proper recognition to Iran and its government. This is the normal recognition that sovereign states are due. Then, through dialogue, the USA will be able to find a way to withdraw with honour.

In all of these appraisals of the situation and of the policy options open to the actors, there is a clear set of ethical moments: Each identifies the actors with good ethical standing (states) and distinguishes them from those that do not have it. The Al Qaeda point of view identifies the USA as a terrorist state, implying that other states are not. Each gives (or hints at) an account of the events leading up to the present state of affairs in which ethical praise and blame are allocated. Each plumps for an option which it portrays as the ethically sound one. These range from recommending withdrawal and putting the blame on the Iraqi government to recommending withdrawal and putting the blame on the USA and UK and, finally, to recommending withdrawal without blame.

[handwritten margin note, right side] How on this is usage piece of diplomatic piss taking!!

[handwritten note, bottom] but that it might not believe is the ethically sound one.

2

GLOBAL ETHICAL PRACTICES

I have argued that the assessments that we have considered above (the BHR, the Parris column, the response of the Bush Administration, the position of the Iraqi government, that of the Al Qaeda supporting press and that of the Iranian government) are all made by participants *within* the practice of sovereign states. The arguments referred to by these appraisers are not simply self-referential ones that only make sense to their own supporters and followers. Instead, they are directed at a global public who, it is hoped, will be convinced by the appraisals put forward. Each assessor seeks to undermine the case put forward by the assessments of the others. The language used by the participants gives us an indication of the shape and form of the practices within which they are constituted.[1] What is the shape of the practice of sovereign states? On what ethical foundations does it rest?

---

1 This is not to deny that there are some people who simply put forward their sets of beliefs in direct confrontation with those of others with different belief systems. But in these encounters there is no argument, there is no claim met by counter-claim and so on. There is no argument about wrongdoing, injustice, lack of equality and so on. There is straight confrontation between groups that do not comprehend one another. Such encounters would be based on pure force. There are few encounters in the modern world of this kind. Even Al Qaeda, which is taken by

Talks about principles of SOSS the
arguments use (for the next few pages)

THE ANARCHICAL SOCIETY OF SOVEREIGN STATES

From a reading of these appraisals looked at in the round, it becomes
apparent then that one of the global practices from within which we
can evaluate the rival appraisals is the society of sovereign states. It
is an anarchical society.[2] The appraisers we have been considering all
identified the key actors in this saga as being states that are entitled
to sovereignty (understood as not being subject to any higher
authority). This norm is recognized in the BHR where it clearly
enunciates the Iraq government's right to rule over Iraq and indicates that the USA by withdrawing will be doing the right thing in
terms of this norm. The opposite of this would be making a case for
imperial rule by the USA asserting the USA's right to rule Iraq as a
colony. No evidence of anything like this is to be found in the docu-
ment. No positive case is made about why the USA is in, or should
be in, Iraq in the first place. The Iranian Foreign Minister is similarly
adamant that the USA should leave Iraq and let it rule itself. The
same view is unambiguously to be found in Parris's article and in
the press sympathetic to Al Qaeda. All the assessments support the
norm of state sovereignty, which implies that states are situated in
an anarchical order.

Closely linked to this is the support that all give to the norm
against intervention in the internal affairs of another sovereign
state. Common to all the positions examined is the recognition that
the USA's military involvement in Iraq is exceptional. It is not normal. There is a recognition, even on the USA side, that this intervention has to be brought to an end. There is a recognition in BHR that
the continued involvement of the USA military forces in Iraq is
harming the USA's international ethical standing. It is not a judgement about the military failing to achieve its targets but a judgement about the mere presence of the USA military (successful or
not) being a problem. This is a tacit admission that intervention is
normally wrong.

many to be a paradigm oppositional movement with no legitimacy whatsoever,
couches its case in arguments that are comprehensible to most participants in
international affairs – arguments to do with USA imperialism, double standards,
exploitation, hypocrisy, human rights abuses against 'unlawful combatants',
religious persecution of Muslims and so on.

2 For a classic elaboration of this society see Bull, 1984.

Closely linked to this in the assessments we have examined is the idea that a sovereign state ought to be self-determining. The BHR suggests that the form of self determination should be democratic in its institutional form.

Similarly, in the readings of the situation we have considered, there is clear reference to a norm according to which groups opposed to the sovereign status and authority of states are to be understood as ethically obnoxious. This is clearly stated in the BHR and in Parris's column. It is implied in the statement by the Iranian government. The Al Qaeda rejection of the 'occupier' is a backhanded support of the sovereignty principle.

In all the reports it is clear that the assessors regard war and violence as normally ethically undesirable and that the pursuit of peace is a better option. Al Qaeda justifies the violence it uses as a special case justified by the exceptional circumstances of occupation and religious persecution. In the reported speeches of Osama Bin Laden he urges violence against the USA and its supporters alleging that they are occupiers bent on the destruction of Islam. He repeatedly calls for the expulsion of the occupier from Palestine. He asserts that the USA will know no peace until its has withdrawn its forces from the Islamic region to the USA (Bin Laden, 2007). The implication is that the norm to be respected is the non-intervention norm. He calls for the establishment of an end to humiliation and the establishment of a just and true government that would promote welfare and security, that would spend the wealth of the country on meeting the needs of the people and not syphoning it off elsewhere. Throughout, it is clear that the moral standing of Al Qaeda itself stems from its opposition to certain wrongful actions of the USA and its allies. The organization does not offer arguments rejecting the system of sovereign states as such but rejects what it claims is wrongful action within the practice of states. It is not revolutionary in the way that Marxist movements were. These sought total transformation of the international political and economic systems. For Al Qaeda the underlying template is still one that recognizes the right of sovereign states to autonomy and self-determination. It recognizes the duty of states to provide welfare for their citizens. It is worth noting, though, that it is utterly opposed to democracy.

There is another technique we can use for getting at the ethical underpinning of the practice within which these assessors are operating. What is left out of the assessments under consideration (what they did not say) is also important for our gaining an understanding of the practice within which the actors are participating. In none of the assessments is there any mention of the salience of international organizations such as the UN, the EU, the Arab League or any other such organization. If these do feature as a component of the practice there is no indication of this here. There is also no reference to the salience of human rights.

In their assessments, then, these actors have given us strong clues about the overall shape of the practice within which their arguments are located. It is one composed of sovereign states existing in an anarchical order. Such an arrangement is not one without order but merely one without an overriding or overarching government. It is one within which the participating units are self-governing states and in which there is a norm of non-intervention in the domestic affairs of other states. It is made clear that there is a norm that in the normal course of events prohibits military engagement in the affairs of another state. There is some indication that it might sometimes be in order to use force in order to establish self-government within the target state. But what is clear is that causing turmoil within the self-governing structures of a sovereign state is considered to be ethically wrong.

A norm is indicated according to which, where once military intervention has taken place, there is a responsibility on the actors in the practice to bring it to an end as soon as possible so that the occupied state might establish self-government for itself. It is clear from all the analyses that, where a state fails to uphold these norms, its international standing in the practice will be undermined and that such an undermining will be a major setback for such a state. In writing such appraisals the authors show themselves to be constructed within this practice. They as participants in the society of sovereign states understand themselves to be interpreting the practice to the other participants in them. This point applies to Al Qaeda as much as to the authors of the BHR.

Once again let us look at what the appraisals do not say. None of them suggest any of the following: that states are ethically entitled to enrich themselves as much as they can at the expense of other states; that states have a right to pursue their self-interest defined as power to the maximum extent they can; that sovereign states are justified in being purely self-seeking; that autarky is what is being sought; that empire is an acceptable goal for any state no matter how powerful; that dishonesty and duplicity are acceptable within this practice; that some states have patriarchal duties towards other less well-developed states; and so on.[3] Instead there is an indication that all states are equally worthy of concern and respect. None of the assessments that I have presented suggested that the insurgent groups, militias, death squads and criminal gangs had in themselves any ethically respectable status in and of themselves. Quite the contrary, they all indicated that the violent activities of such organizations are to be ended as soon as possible. Only Al Qaeda made a case for the value of religious movements using violence in pursuit of its objectives. But at every point it is made clear that the violence is justified on exceptional grounds. It is justified insofar as it is used to expel an occupying force and those who are (or who have been) co-operating with it. To repeat, AQ does not challenge the system of states itself. It talks of punishing states that have become involved in the occupation of states in Islamic areas, but it does not talk of doing away with the system of states itself. Finally, in all the appraisals considered so far there was no mention of any economic actors that have any particularly worthwhile ethical standing.

In summary, then, from evidence internal to this set of assessments we can build a picture of a practice within which the participants, through what they say and do, have constructed a system of sovereign states, within which states have a right to non-intervention in one another's affairs, within which there is a general taboo on military intervention except in exceptional circumstances, in which each participant state has the right to self-determination through its own autonomous government and in which there is a general duty of participant states to care for the maintenance of the whole within which they are participating. In this practice there is a general prohibition on violent uprisings against the government of the day and against sections of the population within the state.

3 It is instructive to read this list and then to read the speeches and publications of Al Qaeda. Many of its arguments derive their force from these criteria. What AQ then does, of course, is link the arguments up to an extreme form of religious fundamentalism. The premises underlying this manoeuvre have no resonance within the practice of states.

There is a rule against empire and colonialism. Most importantly, each state is given a specified area of freedom within which it can be self-governing, but the freedom is constrained by the constitutive limits imposed by the overall constitution of the practice. There is no independent institutional mechanism to determine when a constitutive limit has been breached or not. To be a participant in this practice (to be a sovereign state or a member of such a state) it is required of one that one actually pursue and uphold these rules on an ongoing basis; that each state actively look after the well-being of the anarchical society itself. Failure to do that would damage one's standing as a participant.

EVALUATING RIVAL APPRAISALS

In the previous paragraphs I briefly described the internal indications given to us by the assessors that outlined the ethical components of the practice to which they are appealing in making their assessments. From these we have built a picture of the social formation/practice within which they are acting – a picture of the anarchical society of states. In the language internal to this practice each of the accounts that we have considered gave us a more or less plausible, ethically informed, assessment of the state of play in Iraq at the time and indicated possible directions for future action. Since we ourselves are actors in this practice, the puzzle we now face is: Which of these accounts is the correct one? It is clear that not all of them are compatible with one another. There are severe tensions between them. The BHR claims the ethical high ground for the USA for having deposed a tyrant and having installed democracy. It seeks to lay the blame for the current crisis on the failures of the Iraqi government and the violence of the insurgents and others. Parris, while agreeing that the current violence is perpetrated by these groups, lays the blame for the current state of affairs on the initial occupation by the USA. The critics of the war from within the Middle East do the same. They, too, lay the blame on the USA and the UK for having initiated the war in the first place and for having stayed on in the region as an occupying force.

In the face of these contradictory assessments, what are we to do? We know that any future action in this ongoing war will have to be based on some such appraisal of the situation. Even those of us with but a limited engagement in this war are going to have to make decisions about it. Are we going to remain apathetic about the way in which it develops? Are we going to become actively involved in protesting the ongoing involvement of certain states in the war? Are we going to promote the aims of Al Qaeda? One way or another we shall have to choose between the rival appraisals. Is there a rational way of making such a choice or does our choice have to be arbitrary?

The way forward suggested by the practice model is to delve deeper into this anarchical practice in order to construct the best possible background theory of political ethics which justifies the rules of the practice as a whole. Once we have such a background theory we can use it to decide between the rival interpretations of this particular state of affairs within the overall practice of sovereign states.[4]

In order to build a satisfactory background theory we start by listing the rules, norms and maxims that the participants agree on. Then in a subsequent step we attempt to construct a theory that fits most of these into a more or less coherent ethical theory that displays what values are created or preserved in the practice (in this case, the practice of states). We seek the background ethical theory which best fits the rules, laws, norms and procedures that the participants acknowledge.

IN DEFENCE OF ANARCHY: FREEDOM AND DIVERSITY

To start then: What values are constituted and preserved in the anarchical practice of sovereign states? We are all participants in the society of sovereign states. The primary capacity in which we participate in this practice is as citizens. As such we know the basic features of the practice. We know that it is made up of 193 sovereign states, that the practice is anarchical in form, that the non-intervention norm is crucial within this practice, that the participant

---

4 This manoeuvre is one that we often turn to in all the many social practices within which we participate. When there are disputes about the interpretation of actions in soccer, in church life, in family life, in universities and in political parties (to mention but a few) we engage in a more thoroughgoing discussion of the values that lie behind (or are embedded) in the practice in question. We ask questions such as: What is the essence of soccer? What are the most basic commitments of the church? What are families for? What is the fundamental nature of a university? and so on.

states are entitled to pursue their national interests within certain constraints, that aggression by one state against another is normally wrong, that under certain circumstances going to war is justified and so on. But, although we all know the basic features of this practice, we are unlikely to have ever spent time considering its ethical merits overall. For to think of the ethical merits of a practice is to presuppose that we could arrange things differently if we thought it worthwhile. In the international field, though, for the most part, most of us simply think of the system of states as the way things are. This, we think, is the way that things have turned out rather than an arrangement we have put into place. Where many of us may well have thought of the ethical strengths and weaknesses of the constitutional forms that exist in individual states, evaluating, for example, the merits of different legislative arrangements or different electoral systems, it is unlikely that many have considered the ethical merits of the anarchical arrangements in international relations. Doing so would seem somewhat like dreaming of a utopia, such as, for example, the establishment of a global democracy or a global system based on communist principles. If the current arrangements are simply given and thinking of alternatives is utopian, then it would seem pointless to tackle questions about the ethical underpinning of the anarchical society of states. Doing so would be as silly as discussing the ethical desirability of the moon's orbit around the sun. Ethical questions only arise where the possibility of doing things differently exists. Many consider the option of a new world order as not a real option at all. This line of reasoning is not convincing. This is not how things stand in international politics. For, although we do currently have an anarchical order of sovereign states, things were not always like this. Prior to the existing international arrangements there were others; there were, for example, non-state systems based on tribes and clans (in Africa), pre-modern empire systems (in Egypt and Rome to mention but two), feudal systems linked to an elaborate set of church-based authorities in the Middle Ages and so on. The changes from one system to another may have, in part, been caused by structural features, but the case for pure determinism is difficult to make. Choices by people accounted for a lot of what happened. For example, the developments in Europe after the French Revolution were determined in part by the choices made by Napoleon Bonaparte. Furthermore, not only has there been a history of change in the

Anarchy good as can change things.

international domain but also the contemporary state of affairs is not a static one. In recent times we have seen movement from complex balance of power-type arrangements to a bipolar world, to the current unipolar arrangement. Where once most actors were sovereign states characterized by positive sovereignty, we now have an international order within which many states only possess negative sovereignty.[5] In Western Europe specifically we have witnessed the coming into being of a new form of political arrangement with the appearance of the European Union. The arrangements between the member states of this union are starkly different from those which pertained prior to World War II. Here, once again, what must be stressed is that the coming into being of the EU was a result of specific choice taken by leaders and citizens alike. The general conclusion, then, must be that the international arrangement of states in an anarchical order is not a static given but is a social arrangement which has come about through choices that we have made (Wendt, 1992). This then indicates that a discussion of the ethical merit of the existing system is indeed appropriate. We, the participants in the current arrangement, are able to assess its merits and consider them against the ethical merits of other possible institutional structures.

What values are achieved in our contemporary anarchical society of sovereign states? What set of ethical commitments is embedded in this practice? What ethical background theory is implicit in the practice when seen as a whole? Let us proceed negatively first. What ethical theories could not possibly fit the rules of the practice under scrutiny? Having done this we can then proceed to consider more plausible theories.

Here are some possible background theories which appear to be ruled out ab initio. Given the basic norms of the society of sovereign states that I have outlined above, it is clear that an ethical theory extolling the virtues of empire would not be a contender for an adequate background theory. The rules regarding the autonomy of states and the non-intervention norm could not possibly mesh with a background theory of imperialism. Similarly, the settled norms could not be made to cohere with an ethical theory specifying a social form governed by a ruling elite coming from a particular geographical part of the world or one which was based on race or

5 For a discussion of this notion see Jackson, 1990.

religion. Theories propounding aristocratic rule would also not do. There are many other non-starters that we might think of.

Much more plausible is a background ethical theory which asserts that the prime value of this practice is that it establishes free states within an anarchical society of free states. What is to be valued in this practice is the constitution of a set of actors, states, each of which is within specified limits, free to govern itself. When seen as a social whole what is of value in such an anarchy is that within it each sovereign state is entitled both to decide on its own internal consti- tutional form with regard to its basic structure, legislative system, electoral arrangements and also to pursue its own vision of the good, subject to certain constraints. Some states might pursue liberal policies while others might adopt conservative ones and yet others might strive to be socialist; furthermore, others might opt for Islamic rule while some might opt for a monarchy and so on. In this practice the states are constituted as actors who are responsible for their own successes and their own failures. They are free to experiment with institutions and policies. They are also free to make mistakes within their areas of freedom. Some autonomous actors within this system might decide to develop their states in accordance with a religious creed, while others might be of a more secular orientation. The design of their internal industrial, agricultural, housing, pensions, health, transport, educational and so on policies is up to them and they are responsible for the outcomes of their policy choices in this regard. There is no obligation on all the participant states in this anarchical practice to achieve consensus on any of the policy mea- sures adopted by the others.

It would be implausible for participants in this anarchy of sovereign states to offer, as an ethical ground in support of this arrangement, that it advanced one specific way of life, for example, a socialist one (or a communist one, or a Christian, Islamic or Buddhist one). An arrangement which grants great autonomy to its units is not well suited to putting any single vision of the good into practice.

Over and above establishing a set of autonomous actors with liberties in specified areas, it also seems reasonable[6] to assume that

---

6 'Reasonable' here is taken to mean the achievement of a good fit between the settled rules, norms etc and this justification. No universal claim is being made here about values that are applicable to all people, in all places and for all time (past and future).

the anarchical order of states establishes an arrangement in which a diversity of internal arrangements within states is itself a value for the participants. The value here is the relationship of free states to one another and the diversity which this makes possible. It is a system in which states that are very different from one another nevertheless recognize one another's right to an autonomous existence.[7] It is not far-fetched to imagine that this making possible of a great diversity within a system of states would be an important value in this practice. There is another possibility here which is that the participants might favour a practice which permits diversity on the ground, that anything that stifled this was not likely to work, given the wide variety of tastes, cultures and religions that exist in the world. Either way, the anarchical society of states could be said to be ethically justified because it permits diversity in the lines of action followed by the actors who comprise it.[8]

Having adduced the 'rules of the game' of the society of sovereign states from what the participants say about it, we have now got a rough background theory ready which justifies these rules by extolling the way in which this anarchy constitutes states that are free (sovereign) and by pointing to the way in which it promotes diversity among its members. The background theory is constructed to appeal to those who are actors in this practice and who value their participation in it. In other words, the background theory is to be one that speaks to citizens of sovereign states who value both their citizenship and the sovereignty of their state. It seems difficult to imagine any such person objecting to the background theory that I have offered here. Of course, this background theory would not appeal to anyone who does not value his/her citizenship in a sovereign state.

If the liberty and diversity theory is the best-supporting ethical theory for the anarchical society of states, then this has far-reaching

---

7 If the participants in this practice did not value the diversity that it makes possible, we might expect them to be active in seeking to rule out diversity and impose a uniform practice on all states. If they thought like this we would expect them to be actively seeking to undermine the sovereignty rule and the non-intervention norm.

8 For further discussion of what might be said in defence of anarchy see the section on global civil society (GCS) below.

consequences for what actors in this anarchy are entitled to do. In broad terms, they are required to do what advances these values and to refrain from doing what undermines them. What I would draw attention to here is that this ethical theory sets limits to the means that might be used within this practice. In pursuit of their policies, actors in this anarchy are only entitled to use those means that nurture and protect the core values of liberty and diversity. This rules out attempts to impose one state's values on one or more other states. Actions which may be interpreted as doing this are prima facie wrong.

We are now in a position to evaluate the appraisals of the current conflict in Iraq that were set out above. The test then has to be: Which of the appraisals best accords with the foundational ethical theory that propounds the value of free states in a 'flat' (non-hierarchical) anarchical social form within which states are constituted as free and within which diversity among states is nurtured? Without going into too much detail, let me briefly spell out what such an exercise might produce. In doing this I shall attempt to point to and name the kinds of mistakes that can be made in appraisals. A good appraisal would be one which takes full account of the practice and background theory seen as a dynamic whole within which actors seek to maintain their ethical standing in the face of changing circumstances and challenges from other actors. It would be one which takes into account the ways in which the sequence of interactions between the actors involved either supports or undermines the core values of freedom and diversity.[9]

What are the strengths and weaknesses of the BHR when judged against this background theory? In laying most of the responsibility for the current conflict on the shortcomings of the existing Iraqi government, the BHR failed to give sufficient weight to the value of autonomy which is a core value in the background theory. The flouting of the autonomy value achieved by invading Iraq has led to ongoing resentments and hostilities both within Iraq and more

---

9 The task of making a good appraisal in international relations is not unlike that undertaken by a teacher having to deal with a playground dispute. The pupils involved will often offer partial accounts ('Miss, he hit me first') leaving out salient bits about who was teasing whom or who had stolen whose pocket money and so on. To get the full picture the teacher has to hear and evaluate the rival accounts of the rights and wrongs of the matter, in order to evaluate these in the round.

widely. We, in trying to assess the assessments, have to determine whether the BHR, in discussing the USA engagement in the region, sought to determine whether it was undertaken in such a way that the actors in the region could clearly see that the USA was committed to respecting the non-intervention rule of the global practice of states. An assessor who fully understood the background theory would have taken great care to do this. In the BHR there is no discussion of this issue at all. The fault committed here might be called the fault of omitting relevant ethical history. Good assessments ought to evaluate, from an ethical point of view, the history of conduct by the major parties to a given conflict.[10] Clearly the norm in the practice of states is one of non-intervention. If the norm is to be breached, then good reasons for the exception to the norm must be produced. One would expect the BHR to have referred to these. A close examination of the ethical history to this conflict weakens the plausibility of the BHR considerably. It does not show the USA in a very favourable light. It reveals that the US-led coalition initially justified intervention on the grounds that Iraq had failed to come clean about its programmes engaged in producing weapons of mass destruction (WMD) in terms of its commitments under UN Resolutions. The claims about Iraqi production of WMD subsequently proved to be false. This suggests duplicity on the part of the USA and its allies. Another ground for intervention was one that alluded to close Iraqi links with global terrorist networks, in particular, Al Qaeda. These claims, too, proved to be false. Again this suggests deliberate fabrication of a history of conduct or, at the very least, gross negligence in the production of the history of Iraqi conduct. Subsequent *post hoc* justifications were introduced that alluded to regime change and the promotion of human rights and democracy. But justifications after the event lack cogency and power. A plausible

---

10 A highly contentious issue that I cannot consider in detail here is: Just how far back into the ethical history of a conflict does a good appraisal have to go? Many assessors in writing about the Serbian conflict with Kosovo invoked wrongs committed against Serbs in the 14th century as relevant to appraising the contemporary conflict. This invocation seems excessive. There clearly needs to be some point at which past wrongs are allowed to fall into obscurity. A practice that did not allow for this would condemn itself to perpetual controversy and possible conflict. Yet, ignoring relevant history is clearly a mistake. A balance needs to be struck.

case can be made that the current instability is attributable to actions by the USA and its allies that do not show a history of them being respectful of a central constitutive norm of the practice of sovereign states. The background theory shows this assessment to be a poor one on this score.

On the credit side, the strength of the appraisal offered by the BHR was its recognition of the importance of engaging the other members of the society of states, especially those in the immediate neighbourhood such as Iran and Syria. This shows respect for the autonomy of regional states. It is also in accordance with the deeper ethical commitments embedded in the anarchical society of states which suggests that the maintenance of free states ought to be the concern of all participant states, not merely of any single self-appointed global 'policeman' state. Another strength is the clear commitment in the report to the requirement that the USA withdraw from Iraq so that it, Iraq, might become a free state within the system of free states.

The Parris appraisal displays all the strengths of the BHR but avoids the fault of historical omission. It offers a broader evaluation than did the BHR, in that it examines the contribution both Britain and the USA made to bringing about and aggravating the current conflict. It clearly blames the USA and Britain for this. A weakness of the Parris evaluation is that it does not assess the consequences that would flow from the implementation of its policy prescription, which is a quick withdrawal of the coalition from the region. The background theory suggests that a good evaluation of an international situation, together with its associated set of policy recommendations, must take into account the probable consequences of the proposed set of policy options and subject these to ethical scrutiny. Would the proposed policies, if enacted, bring about more regional and global stability in the system of sovereign states and by so doing promote freedom and diversity? Parris does not consider this question. Furthermore, Parris makes no attempt to situate the evolving situation in Iraq in the nexus of regional relationships between sovereign states. There is no consideration of alternative policy options and the probable consequences of these for the well-being of the ethical whole within which the actors are constituted as sovereign states. Let us call this the fault of ignoring the ethical consequences of an appraisal. Parris's recommendation of withdrawal together with profound apologies does not guarantee a better ethical outcome in terms of these criteria.

The USA policy based on the presidential position paper 'A New Start for Iraq' is clearly supportive of the philosophy behind the system of sovereign states, in that it sets as its goal the establishment of a stable, prosperous Iraq as a free state. But it, too, like the BHR, fails to consider the ethical history of the conflict. This failure makes it difficult to understand the motivations of the belligerents (for example, that many of them see the USA as an illegitimate occupying force) and also makes it difficult to predict what they are likely to do in future. Only a clear understanding of the ethical grievances of the other parties to a conflict can produce sound policies to deal with them. The appraisal, though, does take seriously the whole process of reconstruction and development.

The Iraqi government's appraisal is sound in that it takes into account the ethical history of the conflict. It stresses that this conflict is not of the government's making and that it ought not be blamed for all that is currently happening. But it does not do much to take on the ethical complaints being made by the insurgents, Al Qaeda and so on. This is again the ethical sin of omission – leaving out salient details of the total state of affairs.

The appraisal of Al Qaeda (and the press sympathetic to it) is interesting in that it is in keeping with a major commitment of the system of states which is that foreign occupation of a free state is wrong. It is also critical of the overbearing influence of one state on the many other states in the region. It argues that the USA presence curtails the freedom of the Middle Eastern states. It is critical of the authoritarian rule that is in place in many states, particularly in Saudi Arabia. It claims that authoritarian rulers have been supported in their positions of power by the presence of the USA in the region over a long period. Here we see that, although Al Qaeda is not a recognized legitimate actor in the system of sovereign states, nevertheless, in the appraisals it makes, it refers to well-known criteria in this practice. It also refers to Islamic religious criteria and portrays the USA as a crusader nation. The implication is that the USA is engaged in a religious war against Islam. If this were true this would show up the USA to be acting contrary to the diversity commitment embodied in the practice of states in terms of which different states are entitled to pursue different religious traditions within the confines of their own sovereign jurisdictions. *Eius regio cuius religio* is one of the founding principles of the system of sovereign states dating back to the time of the Treaty of Westphalia.[11] If this charge could be shown to be true, then it would show the USA to be engaged in a religious war which would undermine a fundamental principle of the present day practice of states. On the debit side of the AQ appraisal is the fact that it runs roughshod over the ethical constraints required by the international practice of states on the means to be used in pursuing one's ethical goals. There is little or no attempt to evaluate the means used against the core values of the practice.

Finally, if we consider the appraisal offered by Iran, we can see that it is committed to establishing Iraq as a viable free state, that it is committed to getting the states of the region involved in seeking a solution. It also acknowledges that what is ethically required is to get the USA out of Iraq. All of these are in keeping with the underlying ethic of practice of states extolling the virtues of freedom and diversity. What is lacking is any ethical evaluation of its own role in fomenting the current wave of unrest in Iraq. It is clearly being less than candid about what it has done to promote the conflict and about what the ethical issues in play are. Here again we see an instance of what might be called 'the sin of omission'.

If we consider this brief and superficial appraisal of the appraisals, what has emerged is that several of the flaws that have come to light relate to omissions: omitting the relevant ethical history to a conflict, omitting a consideration of the ethical consequences of recommended courses of action and omitting to evaluate the ethicality of the policy mechanisms being produced. What we have encountered are actors who put forward assessments that are partial in that they omit ethically relevant elements. A strong case may be made that the assessments are produced with both strategic and tactical concerns in mind. Assessors do not set out to make their assessments from an ethically neutral platform. Each assessor comes to the task in hand with ethical baggage – they come to the task carrying ethical burdens imposed on them by the previous assessments of others. In their own assessments of a current situation they then attempt to hide the ethical weaknesses of their own cases. Each appraiser

---

11 For an interesting discussion of Westphalia see Krasner 1995.

attempts to make his/her/its appraisal into the one that carries the day, the one that wins the ethical argument in the teeth of previous hostile assessments made by others.[12]

The ways in which accounts of international states of affairs may be deficient include:

- omission of ethically relevant features of the history that lead up to the existing state of international affairs (e.g. leaving out of the history of blame and responsibility among the participants, including one's own history)
- deceit of one kind or another (e.g. lying, bluffing, pretending about who was responsible for what)
- demonstrated hypocrisy (e.g. upholding one criterion in one appraisal only to ignore its relevance in the next comparable case)
- deliberate use of double standards (e.g. giving an account in terms of a standard of civilization in one case, but ignoring it in the next one).

I shall say more later about the kinds of errors we ought (and do) look for when evaluating appraisals of given states of affairs in international relations.

Why do actors present appraisals that are partial in the ways that I have outlined? The obvious answer is that they do this because they think they can get away with it. They believe that the audience to which the assessment is directed will not notice the omissions and consequently their own ethical standing will remain high. In

12 It is important at this point not to slip back into thinking in realist terms that the ethical arguments are simply used as window-dressing for conduct taken for other reasons – not to slip back into thinking that ethical appraisals are mere rationalizations for actions pursued for other reasons such as the pursuit of power. The ethical accounts are what determine the actions that follow. The ethical dimensions of the appraisals are not some unimportant 'add-on'. The short statement must be that appraisals are not window-dressing but are the basis on which actions are undertaken. All actions are taken on the basis of some ethically informed appraisal of an existing state of affairs. Thus, any successful criticism of the appraisals will result in an undermining of the standing of the appraiser and the undermining of any power manoeuvres he wishes to make. Of course, from time to time actors might decided to be duplicitous. They might decide to attempt to hide the real appraisals that inform their actions. They might attempt to do this by producing a rationalizing 'cover up' of the account on which their actions are based.

particular, very powerful collective actors, such as states, do it in the belief that their control of the media is such that they can simply manipulate people into accepting their appraisals and that they can prevent criticisms reaching the ears of the audience they are addressing.[13] The effort and resources that are ploughed by international actors into controlling the message is a clear indication of just how vulnerable to such criticisms these actors are. When the lies and half-truths that the coalition produced in the run-up to the second war in Iraq became known, the standing (and hence political power both at home and abroad) of the Bush and Blair governments was significantly eroded. This in turn influenced the course of events in the region, the domestic politics of the USA and the UK, and the political futures of both George W. Bush and Tony Blair.

What we have been doing in this section is not a second-order activity. On the analysis that I have given, producing an appraisal is itself an action that can be appraised as ethically sound (or not). Thus, the production of an appraisal is an act in the international realm that can be ethically evaluated. The analysis being given here must be included in this category. The discipline of IR consists of appraisals of appraisals. The presentation of weak assessments must be understood as an ethical wrong within the practice of sovereign states.

In this section I have illustrated, by using the current war in Iraq as an example, how an ethics-centred form of social analysis might work. As a point of departure we considered a set of rival evaluations of the history and conduct of the war. These evaluations contained in them conflicting suggestions about future policy directions that might be taken. I then showed how social practice theory (constitutive theory) gives us a vantage point from which to evaluate such contending claims in terms of the standards that are internal to the practice within which the appraisals were presented.

---

13 An extreme example of this is to be found in the assessment of international affairs that President Mugabe presented to his citizens in Zimbabwe. Since he has near total control of the domestic media he can present biased accounts of the history of ethical action that has led to the current state of affairs in Zimbabwe. In the accounts produced by his government, blame is uniformly placed on the perfidy of the British government. His assessments leave out a lot of ethically relevant information about the causes of the internal crisis, such as governmental incompetence and corruption. He relies on the inability of the domestic audience to get hold of the relevant information that would undermine his case.

Our consideration of the war in Iraq led us to focus on one major international global practice, the system of sovereign states. Our evaluation of the appraisals given has been in terms of the embedded ethic of this practice alone. Were this the only global practice, we could now turn to unpacking the finer details of its ethical structure. However, the society of sovereign states is not the only global practice. It is not the only practice that includes within itself, as participants, nearly everyone everywhere. There is another worldwide practice in which we all participate, global civil society (GCS). This, like all other social practices has internal to it a set of ethical components. That most people are simultaneously participants in both the society of sovereign states and global civil society makes it considerably more difficult to appraise our international activities properly. An adequate, ethically informed, appraisal of any set of activities in the global sphere has to take account of the interrelationship between the two practices, paying particular attention to the ethical underpinnings of each.

Before we can get to grips with these complexities it is necessary to set out the basic features of global civil society, together with an analysis of the ethic embedded in it. What makes an analysis of the relationship between these two practices particularly interesting is that both of them are anarchical in form. Yet, in spite of this similarity, and in spite of complex and close relationships between the two, they are distinct and different social formations. Each needs to be understood in its own terms before the interrelationships between them can be discussed.

THE ANARCHICAL SOCIETY OF CIVILIANS: GLOBAL CIVIL SOCIETY

In order to introduce the discussion of global civil society, I shall follow the form of argument that I used in discussing the society of sovereign states. Here, once again, I shall start by setting out a set of conflicting appraisals of a specific set of interactions to be found in the current war in Iraq. Here, once again, my claim will be that at the heart of such conflicting appraisals are ethical disputes. These are disputes in which the actions and arguments of the participating parties can be understood as attempts to establish the ethical superiority of their actions and to undermine, from an ethical point of view, the actions of their opponents. Understanding them as such is crucial to gaining a good understanding of what is happening in this sphere. Having such an understanding is essential to any subsequent action.

In order to make my case I shall examine the language within which the dispute is couched, in order to determine the form of the practice within which the dispute is taking place. A key question will be: Does the language indicate the existence of a global practice or is it geographically limited or limited in some other way? Having made the case that a global civil society exists, in a subsequent step I shall tease out the ethic embedded in this global practice and I shall show how this may be used to evaluate the rival appraisals with which the exercise started.

Evidence of the existence of a global civil society, distinct from the practice of states, is to be found in the language used by the partici-pants in the current war in Iraq.[14] The core evidence for the existence of GCS is to be found in the language of human rights that is used in many different and often conflicting appraisals of various activities taking place there. It is used by members of the intervening powers, by outsiders not directly involved in the conflict and by local people in the line of fire, as it were. Although the human rights discourse covers a whole range of different issue areas, one particularly recurrent one emerges in discussions about private military companies (PMCs), sometimes referred to as private security companies (PSCs).[15] Let us look more closely at the conflicting appraisals of PMCs and PSCs.[16]

---

14 As indicated earlier, there is nothing particularly significant about looking for the evidence of a global practice in this location. If, as I claim, the practice is global, then evidence of its existence ought to be manifest everywhere. But since we have been considering Iraq it seems sensible to use the same example again. This will make it easier at a later stage to see how simultaneous participation in both practices complicates our task when appraising what is happening in that part of the world.

15 Human rights-related issues also emerge in discussions about the war being an example of what has come to be known as a 'New War'. They also arise in connec-tion with the use of private companies that carry out interrogations of captured enemy combatants. Human rights come to the fore in discussions of the role of private corporations in the reconstruction and development operations taking place in the region. On a much wider scale there are rights issues that emerge in discussions of the operation of the free market in the war-torn areas in Iraq and elsewhere in the world.

16 From now on I shall use the terms interchangeably.

PRIVATE MILITARY COMPANIES: CONTESTED APPRAISALS

It is increasingly the case that governments involved in military action abroad make use of PMCs. In Iraq there has been a spectacular increase in their use, both by the coalition and by the current Iraqi government. Similarly, corporations who operate in this and other dangerous parts of the world are making more and more use of PSCs. There is widespread agreement amongst scholars, politicians and the general international public that these collective actors are becoming increasingly important in this conflict. A fortiori there is agreement that the activities of such organizations need to be understood, explained and evaluated. In short, their activities need to be appraised. A veritable explosion of scholarly activity has emerged to tackle this task.

In the public discussion about the role of PMCs in this conflict (and in other conflicts worldwide), there are two starkly opposed ways of understanding them. In the first of these, PMCs are portrayed as legitimate private companies offering services to satisfy a widespread range of legitimate security-related demands. On this view, both in Iraq and elsewhere there are individuals, governments and corporations that require the provision of security to which they are entitled. The services required cover activities that include: providing for the personal security of key personnel; the provision of security for those engaged in the physical reconstruction of damaged infrastructure (water, electricity, telephone networks, sewage systems and so on); the guarding of key installations (airports, ports, railways, roads, pipelines); training of military and police personnel; training of the general public in security related matters; the provision of security for companies that transport cash to shops, banks etc; the providing of security for the private property of individuals and many others. There is, so this account goes, nothing wrong or criminal about the demand for the security services listed above. The demand for these services is found everywhere, both in domains of peace and in areas of conflict. These demands have been met by specialist private companies, small and large. Some are listed companies.

On this view, we are to understand private military companies (PMCs) as a subcategory of PSCs. They provide very similar services, but they satisfy a demand linked to military functions. In recent wars, states have increasingly contracted PMCs to undertake security-related work that has traditionally been done by the states' military forces. The functions served are similar to those described above, but the circumstances within which they are called upon to operate are often more unstable, unpredictable and dangerous. Typical of PMCs are the following: Blackwater, Erinys, L3, Aegis Defence Services, MPRI, Global Risk Strategies, ArmorGroup and Custer Battles.[17] These corporations have an interest group lobby called the International Peace Operations Association (IPOA). According to the appraisal being set out here, we are to understand PSCs and PMCs as meeting a legitimate demand that has emerged in the international market for services of this kind. Contracts are established and carried out. Both parties to such contracts stand to benefit.

These market exchanges are understood to be subject to the normal ethical constraints operative in capitalist markets for goods and services. The actors are rights holders who may be individual men and women or collective actors such as corporations. Rights holders have available to them a whole range of legitimate transactions, most of which involve the making of contracts for various purposes. What has to be avoided is the abuse of individual rights. For example, contracts based on force or fraud are not considered legitimate. The PSCs and PMCs, being newcomers to the market, are all acutely aware of the constraints under which they are to operate. In their literature and on their websites these companies are careful to declare themselves obedient to the ethical requirements of this practice.[18]

---

17 For a much longer list of such organizations see the website at: http://www.globalsecurity.org/military/world/para/pmc-list.htm.

18 For example, Blackwater, the largest PMC in the world, has a mission statement which declares: 'Blackwater is committed to supporting U.S. national security strategy, global justice, and the rule of law. We dedicate ourselves to providing ethical, efficient, and effective turnkey solutions that both protect America and those who are defenceless, and give them a free voice the world over.' See the website at: http://www.blackwaterusa.com/about/missionstatement.asp.

The organization also has an explicit ethical commitment spelled out as follows: 'Blackwater supports increased accountability and transparency in the private security industry. We conduct ourselves and our business with honor and integrity. As members of and partners with the International Peace Operators Association, we accept and daily abide by our collective Code of Conduct http://www.ipoaonline.org/code.htm.'

In sharp contrast to this kind of appraisal are those which depict PSCs and especially PMCs as little better than companies of mercenaries – hired guns that are out to sell their services to the highest bidder. On this account such actors are out to serve their own interests. They are not bound by ethical standards, their activities are not transparent and they are not accountable to anyone but the buyers of their services.[19] In these alternative accounts their actions are roundly condemned on a number of different counts, but at the heart of all the criticisms is the claim that the operation of PMCs pose a threat to human rights. In other words, this appraisal appeals to the same set of criteria as the pro-PMC account we considered above. Those offering the negative appraisal of PMCs claim that military action aimed at upholding human rights is not likely to achieve that outcome when the military function is carried out by private contractors. The reasons put forward for this assertion usually include the following: private companies are more likely to favour the interests of those employing them than the human rights of all; the market mechanism is not one that will ensure that human rights are respected all round; PMCs are likely to be rights-abusing in their conduct because they are not accountable to civilians in general but only to the principal actor that employed them; where the employer is a government of a state, the PMCs are not subject to the same processes of accountability to which the government itself is subject; in general, PMCs are not well regulated; and so on. The policy option offered by such critics is that military forces and the use of military force ought always to be under the control of a state or a group of states. A further variation on this theme is that such companies actually help the states that employ them to avoid their responsibilities.[20]

Here then, once again, we have conflicting appraisals of the same phenomenon. On the one hand, are those who argue that we are to understand PMCs as legitimate actors in the global free market, as actors who promote the protection of human rights, while, on the other hand, are those who claim that the operation of these companies positively threatens human rights. Each understands,

---

19 For a typical example of this kind of appraisal see Beernink, 2005.
20 For a concise statement of a list of ethical charges to be made against the use of PMCs see Christian, 2005.

explains and evaluates such companies in starkly different ways. The dispute between these rival appraisals is important both for those directly involved in this sphere of operation and for the rest of us who are called upon to either support the activities of these groups or to oppose them. Which account we support will determine what we do. Once again it is important to stress that the evaluation given is not an 'add-on' to some neutral description of the activities of PMCs; any account of the actions of PMCs will be an appraisal which includes an ethical component. There is no neutral description of what they do.

How are we to evaluate these rival appraisals of PMCs both as they operate in Iraq and generally? As before, our initial task must be to describe the practice within which the conflicting appraisals are located.[21] We do this by noting the common language used by the appraisers and their audience. In particular, we should pay attention to the area of argument in which they show themselves to be vulnerable. That is, we pay particular attention to the allegations to which the parties feel obliged to make defensive responses. These will reveal to us the embedded values in GCS. The ones that participants are wary of undermining for fear of undermining their own standing in GCS. Overall, we need to pay attention to the whole complex of concepts, rules, and procedures that we refer to in order to make sense of what the appraisers say.

Here is an example of the language used by one of the participants in GCS. One PMC chosen at random, ArmorGroup, appraises itself and what it does as follows. The language used is typical for this type of actor:

> For over 25 years ArmorGroup has been recognised as a leading provider of defensive, protective security services to national governments,

---

21 It is important to stress once again that, if there were no common practice within which these rival assessments of PMCs are offered, then we would be dealing with an encounter rather than an interaction or argument. Without the common practice it would be an encounter between parties whose discourses were incomprehensible to one another. Here we would simply have to note the encounter, there would be no possibility of scholars arguing the merits of the opposing views. The debate about how best to understand PMCs is not like this – it is not a merely an event of mutual incomprehension.

multinational corporations and international peace and security organisations operating in hazardous environments.

ArmorGroup is headquartered in London and listed on the London
Stock Exchange.

ArmorGroup has over 9,000 highly trained and experienced
employees and long-term operations in 38 countries. Over the past two
years it has supported its clients in over 160 countries across the Middle East, Africa, North and South America, the CIS and central Asia.[22]

In this case the language indicates that the company is a provider
of services to clients around the world and that it is a listed company. We who understand the passage from AmorGoup represented
above know that anyone who understands the quote understands
something about that complex set of terms, rules and procedures
that we know as the global capitalist market. Crucial to this are
notions such as private property, contract, money, firm, credit, debt,
price, banking, exchange, interest, interest rates, wealth, stock
exchange, shares (equity), share market and many others. People
who understand the market understand how these terms relate to
one another in a complex social discourse. Key to understanding all
of these is an understanding of the notion of a rights holder. We
know a market to consist of at least this; it is a place where people
who have property rights bargain with one another and make contracts to buy and sell what they have. The notion of being a rights
holder is central here. It would not be possible to make sense of any
of the other concepts listed above without an understanding of what
is involved in being a rights holder.

The claims made by the PMCs also refer to a wider practice that
stretches beyond the market, narrowly conceived as an economic
institution. The leading PMCs openly declare their commitment to
human rights and to a slew of instruments that protect them. For
example, IPOA, an umbrella organization that represents many
PMCs, in its mission statement, explicitly states that all its members
are committed to the protection of human rights and all the major
international instruments that have been instituted do protect
them.[23] The Head of IPOA travels the world inviting scrutiny of the

22 http://www.armorgroup.com/aboutus/ (accessed 20 March 2007).
23 See its website at http://ipoaonline.org/php/.

member companies of IPOA. He invites scrutiny in terms of a standard (and rather full) set of human rights requirements. In this book I am calling the social practice within which people recognize one another as holders of equal sets of fundamental human rights 'global civil society' (GCS) and the participants in this society 'civilians'. Civilians recognize one another as holders of first-generation rights that include, amongst others, the rights of the person, such as the right not to be killed, tortured, assaulted, the right to free speech, the right to freedom of association, academic freedom, freedom of conscience, the right to freedom of movement, together with rights to own property including having a property right to own one's own labour power.[24]

Crucially, the society within which civilians enjoy these rights is understood to be boundaryless. Those who participate in this discourse do not speak in ways which suggest that people have human rights in one place, for example, in a particular state with clear boundaries, but not in other places. Rights holders do not speak of becoming rights-less as they cross specified boundaries. Instead, the claim is that the society of rights holders is global. Rights holders have their sets of basic individual rights, wherever they happen to be, and they continue to have their rights no matter where they go. Even if they go to autocratic states that do not protect their individual rights, civilians everywhere still consider that they have their rights. Of course, their rights might not be equally well protected in all places at all times. In some areas of the world rights are well protected and in others they are not. But the general point holds the participants in global civil society consider that the anarchical society within which they hold those rights has no borders.

Beyond this borderlessness, rights holders in global civil society consider that all men and women everywhere are participants in

24 I do not present this list as exhaustive. It is illustrative. There are interesting and ongoing disputes among civilians as to what rights should be included on the list. I am also not concerned in this book to provide any empirical or metaphysical arguments grounding the set of human rights that civilians take themselves to have. My point is simply that, as things currently stand, most people are participants in a global civil society within which they constitute one another as rights holders. They do this by making rights claims for themselves and recognizing such claims from others.

GCS. Their evidence for thinking this includes the fact most people in most places would claim to have human rights. There are no significant groupings who say of themselves that they have no human rights. Also, most people in most places are in some way or another participants in the global economic market as buyers or sellers of commodities, as buyers or sellers of labour and in many other ways. As participants they claim rights for themselves, the most important of which are the right to own property and the right to make contracts. Other key rights required for the global market are the right to form associations, the right to protect ones rights and so on.

Those who articulate an alternative understanding of the PMCs' role in conflict situations also use language that makes it clear that they understand the companies to be acting within the context of the global market and GCS more generally. Their understanding of what PMCs are and what they do demonstrates that they, too, fully understand the complex set of concepts, rules and procedures that make up the global market and global civil society. The criteria that inform their criticisms of PMCs are the same ones that IPOA professes to uphold. However, these critics make the claim that PMCs as they currently operate do not advance the human rights values implicit in GCS, but undermine them.

Here again, as earlier, I wish to stress that, in order to understand what is going on in the Middle East at the moment, one has to understand the crucial role played by PSCs and PMCs. But in order to do this one has to assess the rival understandings that are being put forward. Doing this requires that they be understood *within* the discourse of GCS. At the heart of this rivalry are the ethical dimensions that we have been discussing. Each, in putting forward its assessment, seeks to undermine the ethical standing of those putting forward the counterview. Thus, those making the case for PSCs and PMCs in the Middle East are seeking to portray what they do as making a strong contribution to maintaining the ethical values implicit in free market practices and in wider civil society generally. Through the act of appraisal they seek to portray these actors in a very positive ethical light. We the audience are asked to share this evaluation and are asked to base our future actions on it.

In contrast, those who offer the alternative anti-PSC and PMC appraisal are seeking to undermine the moral standing of PMCs.

They seek to tar them as mercenary soldiers of fortune, as the 'dogs of war' who are not accountable to civilians in general, but only to their paymasters. Here, as before, we can see that the acts of ethical appraisal and counterappraisal are key to understanding and explaining the activities of these organizations. Here, again we can see how this first step of appraisal is the primary one on which all future policy-making and implementation will and must be based. Thus, it follows that if we are to be active in the practice at all, we must evaluate these rival claims. In order to participate we have to make an assessment of these assessments.

Which of these diametrically opposed appraisals is the correct one? In terms of the approach to international relations that I am putting forward here, we are not, at this point, simply faced with the option of an arbitrary choice as to which of these two general forms of appraisal is correct. Instead, we know the parties to the dispute are, with us, co-participants in a global practice that we are able to investigate with a view to seeking guidance in deciding which interpretation of PMCs is to be preferred. Using practice theory requires of us that we attempt to set out the broad shape of GCS and then construct the best possible background ethical theory that supports its specific shape. We shall then be able to use the background theory to evaluate the rival claims about the role of PMCs in international affairs.

IN DEFENCE OF ANARCHY: FREEDOM AND DIVERSITY

If we look at the concepts, rules and procedures of GCS what ethical values might it be said to promote? GCS, like the system of sovereign states (SOSS) that we discussed above, has as a primary feature that it is anarchical in form. What this means is that it, like the SOSS, is a dispersed practice (Schatzki, 1996). In both practices the participants interact with one another in terms of a common set of rules, but without a central authority. The anarchical structures, by definition, are 'flat' rather than hierarchical. In global civil society the rights-holding participants, the civilians, are entitled to order their lives as they deem fit without guidance or constraint from any central authority. They simply have to refrain from abusing any of the fundamental rights of the other civilians in the practice. Of course, rights holders might decide amongst themselves to form associations of one kind or another. Such associations might be set up with a clear hierarchical structure, but this does not fundamentally affect the basic form of GCS as an anarchical system because the formation of such associations does not affect the status of the participants in GCS, who remain rights holders throughout the creation, dissolution and recreation of any number of associations.[25]

Let me stress again that anarchical societies must be understood as social institutions with a distinct social form. The word 'anarchical' must not be read as indicating the absence of a social institution. It does not indicate that the participating entities (rights holders and states) relate to one another in a haphazard way. It does not indicate that they interact without adhering to any social rules. In anarchical societies the actors are strictly constrained by the rules of the social practice with its anarchical form. For example, in GCS, a wealthy rights holder such as Bill Gates is not entitled to do what he wishes *vis-à-vis* his co-participants. He is bound by the rights-conferring rules of the practice which dictate that he must recognize and respect the rights of his fellow rights holders in GCS. His rights are on a par with those of all other participants. Of course, the use that he has made of his rights in the free market have made him a wealthy man and he is in a good position to use his wealth to influence others to do his bidding. But the wealth does not give him a right to interfere with or override the rights of others, although it will certainly give him the power to do so.

---

25 In a similar fashion the members of the society of states are located as actors in a dispersed practice. Each state is located in a 'flat' institutional form without central government. The sovereign states are entitled to pursue what policies they wish provided only that they respect one another's sovereign rights – respect one another's freedoms. What is fundamental for each participant state is that the other states accord them recognition as sovereign free states. Here, too, as in GCS, the participants are, of course, free to form associations of states for different purposes. Some states might get together to create a customs union such as the South African Customs Union (SACU) or the North American Free Trade Association (NAFTA). The members of the anarchical society of states can form collective security arrangements such as the UN system. These unions might have clearly defined centralized authority structures, but this in no way detracts from the participants' fundamental ethical status as sovereign free states who are free to disassociate from the SACU, NAFTA or the UN and to form new associations as and when they see fit to do so.

Given that the anarchical form is, indeed, a social institution and thus one that can be changed, it is important to ask: What, from an ethical point of view, can be said in support of social institutions within an anarchical form? What background ethical theory justifies them? Is there anything in general that can be said in its defence of social institutions with this shape?[26] These are important questions because, given that an anarchy is a social institution, we participants need to consider whether, from an ethical point of view, there is good reason to maintain this social formation, rather than adopt another form of institution, centralized, hierarchical ones, for example. We also need a point of view from which to generate answers to difficult ethical and political problems when they arise. We need a point of view from which to solve the 'hard cases'.

There is an impressive list of things that can be said in support of institutions that are anarchical in shape. Taken together they form a comprehensive justificatory theory which provides the participants with good reason for nurturing this structure and seeking to defend it from dangers. This theory will be of great use in deciding hard cases.

First, the anarchical form is one in which the participants are constituted as free actors. In GCS, rights holders adhere to a set of social rules which specify that they grant to one another a set of fundamental human rights. It seems reasonable to assume that rights holders value the anarchy for precisely the reason that in it they are constituted as having a specific set of freedoms. It would be difficult for those claiming rights for themselves to reject the notion that the anarchy as a whole is to be valued for the way in which it constitutes people as free.

Second, in this anarchical society, the participants, as rights holders, are each free to pursue their own vision of the good. They may do this subject only to the constraint that they do not infringe the rights of other rights holders to do the same. Thus, some rights holders might set out to live an ascetic life dedicated to meditating on the good works of Jesus, Buddha or the Prophet Mohammed, while others pursue an ideal devoted to the pursuit of carnal pleasure.

26 The question here is analogous to one that might be asked about federal institutional structures: Is there anything that can be said in a general way about the merits of federal social institutions?

Some might seek to dedicate their lives to the advancement of a specific national group, such as the Croatian nation, where others might seek meaning for their lives in multicultural forums.[27] This is similar to the point we made in considering the anarchical society of states within which sovereign states are entitled to use their sovereign freedoms to pursue very different ideas of the national good. Some states might commit to the pursuit of a social-welfarist form of life (Norway, Sweden); others might seek a strictly capitalist form (the USA), while others might strive to set up a communist state (North Korea); yet others might seek to pursue the cultural purposes of a particular nation (Croatia). It is hard to imagine any other social form enabling all these different kinds of states to pursue their divergent national interests. Here once again, each state is free, subject only to the extent that it does not interfere with the sovereign rights of other states to do the same. Again it is difficult to see how states who claim sovereignty for themselves could deny that this is an ethical good produced by the anarchical society as a whole.

In passing it is worth noting that there are two different ways of reading this value of an anarchical system – the value, that is, that it allows for the co-existence of free actors each pursuing different ideas of the good and different ideas of its own self-interest. On the first interpretation, the anarchical form is to be commended for providing rules of co-existence for a number of actors who, without that set of rules, might soon fall into violent and ongoing conflict with one another. This is a prudential or pragmatic reason for supporting this kind of arrangement.[28] According to a second interpretation, the

27 Robert Nozick makes this point in a particularly powerful way. He asks whether there could possibly be one kind of life that would accommodate all of the following: 'Wittgenstein, Elizabeth Taylor, Bertrand Russell, Thomas Merton, Yogi Berra, Allen Ginsberg, Harry Wolfson, Thoreau, Casey Strengel, The Lubavitcher Rebbe, Picasso, Moses, Baba Ram Dass, Gandhi, Sir Edmund Hillary, Raymond Lubitz, Buddha, Frank Sinatra, Columbus, Freud, Normal Mailer, Ayn Rand, Baron Rothschild, Ted Williams, Thomas Edison, H. L. Mencken, Thomas Jefferson, Ralph Ellison, Bobby Fischer, Emma Goldman, Peter Kropotkin, you and your parents.' Clearly not. What we need, he says, is a framework which will allow a diversity of people with different ideas of the good and of utopia to live together (Nozick, 1974, p. 310).

28 Terry Nardin has provided a defence of the anarchical society of states along these lines (Nardin, 1983, Introduction).

anarchical form has merit not merely for pragmatic reasons referring to what it prevents (conflict, violence etc), but for the positive
reason that it is a social form that positively promotes diversity.
Actors in such a form are encouraged to pursue their diverse life
plans. On this view, participants in the anarchical system might
regard living in a social arrangement that promotes diversity as
a positive social value in itself. They might regard living in such a
social order to be richer, more fulfilling and more interesting than
living in a social order that advances a more narrowly defined set of
social goals. It seems fair to assume that those millions of people who
become international tourists for portions of each year are motivated
by just such a consideration. To participate in international
tourism is to participate in the enjoyment of a plural world that
the anarchical form of both GCS and system of sovereign states
makes possible.

Third, anarchical societies not only allow for pluralism but they
nurture it.[29] By respecting the rights of the other actors to pursue
their own versions of the good, participants are actually encouraging
the emergence of a diverse universe of actors. To be granted a set of
freedoms – to be constituted as a free actor – is to be invited to decide
how to make use of the freedoms one has been constituted as having.

Fourth, not only does the anarchical form constitute actors as free
and invite the development of a plurality of different outlines,
policies and plans for the good life, it also encourages change,
experimentation and development. The civilians and citizens who
participate in GCS and the society of sovereign states respectively
are not presented with a 'one-off' chance to adopt a vision of the
good to guide their lives – a vision that they then have to commit to
for ever. Instead, through being recognized as free actors with the
right to choose their life plans, civilians and citizens are given the
opportunity to experiment with different ways of being in the world.
For example, an individual civilian might start out practising Chris-
tianity in a conventional church, might then be 'born again' in a
fundamentalist movement and then end up living a highly secular
life outside of any religious context (possibly in San Francisco). In

---

29 Such a point has been advanced by Joseph Raz in Raz, 1986. Although Raz was
   discussing freedom within states, his point seems to be applicable more generally.

the society of states an example is provided by the citizens of Tanzania who, as citizens in a sovereign state, were given the chance to experiment with a form of African socialism called *ujama*. They subsequently abandoned this for a more conventional approach to democracy and development. In doing these things, civilians and citizens will invariably engage in a process of social experimentation. After a time, the people in question might find that a certain form of life appears to be less satisfying than was originally anticipated. In social institutions that are anarchic in form, actors are free to start again and choose different goals for their lives. A permutation of this reason for supporting the anarchical form of social practice is that in it this process of social experimentation is not only open to actors within the context of their own lives and choices, as civilians or citizens, but it also gives them the opportunity of watching how the decisions taken by other actors pan out. So a state wishing to develop in a social-welfarist direction might learn useful lessons from close observation of the experiences of other states who have tried similar policies. In Africa a sovereign state such as Zimbabwe has experimented in a rather dramatic way with policies aimed at the forcible redistribution of land among its citizens. Neighbouring civilians and citizens are in a good position to learn valuable lessons through close observation of the debacle unfolding there.

Fifth, a further strength of anarchical systems is a utilitarian one. The utility of anarchical systems flows from the way in which their structure renders them invulnerable to a certain kind of attack. Their strength is the opposite of that contained in the old adage *Ex unitate vires* (From unity comes strength). An anarchy, by having no central command structure, does not have a single locus of authority that, once defeated by an enemy, signifies the defeat of the whole. Instead, the very dispersedness of an anarchical practice is its strength. An attack and defeat at one point leaves the rest intact. Thus, were an enemy to threaten the rights of civilians in one part of GCS, for example, in that portion covered by Zimbabwe, that would still leave the rest of global society in place to continue as a freedom-constituting zone for civilians elsewhere. Similarly, in the society of states, if an enemy were to deprive several states in South Asia of their autonomy, this would not threaten the anarchical society as a whole. No doubt the member states of the anarchy who were not defeated by such attacks would be furious about what had been done to the society, but they would still be intact and able to regroup in order to reverse the setback.

Sixth, a unique feature of anarchical societies is that the defence of the whole is achieved through the self-defence actions of the component actors. Although anarchies are not vulnerable to the same attack on the centre that hierarchical organizations are, they are nevertheless, like all social arrangements, open to threat. Like other social orders they might need to be defended from time to time from internal or external threats – they might be required to act in defence of anarchy. Since anarchies have no central government and no central defence force, the task of defence falls to the individual members. It falls to individual civilians in GCS and to individual states in the society of states. It falls to the rights holder to make a decision about how best to defend him- or herself. The same applies to individual states. What we need to notice here, though, is that through self-defence the individual actors are contributing to the defence of the whole. In an anarchy, provided that the defensive actions do not infringe the rights of other actors, self-defence is an act in the public interest of the whole. So, for example, when any single state in the anarchy of sovereign states defends itself against aggression, it is not only defending itself but is defending the whole system of sovereign states. This might not be the actor's conscious intention, but it is the effect of an actor's obedience to the self-defence rule that is constitutive of anarchical societies. Of course, from time to time an individual actor within an anarchical practice will not be strong enough to defend himself/herself/itself. In such cases actors have to form defensive associations. In the context of civil society such a self defence association might, with time, come to resemble a minimal state.[30] In the context of a society of sovereign states, when a number of states form such a defensive association this could take the form of a defensive treaty-based alliance such as NATO.

A seventh feature of ethical significance in anarchical societies is that they are open. An actor joins them simply by learning how to obey the constitutive rules. Would-be participants do not need to apply for membership. Thus, there are no selection committees to

---

30 The hidden-hand process through which this might come about has been described by Nozick (Nozick 1974, passim).

veto individual applications or that could institute unfair and discriminatory admission policies.[31] A point closely related to this is that in this kind of society there is similarly no unique single authority that can expel members. The rules of anarchies are policed by their members.

An eighth feature of such societies is that because they have no central law-making facility the constitutive rules of anarchies can only change incrementally through the individual actions of participants over time. Gradually, through customary usage, participants in anarchies may come to recognize a new rule or changes to the old ones.

Finally, and this is a point of great importance, anarchies make possible a certain kind of politics and then set clear limits to it. In an anarchy, the participating rights holders are entitled to discuss with one another suggestions for changing the social arrangements which exist between them and to set about implementing these. However, as always, the constitutive rules of these anarchies specify that political action must not infringe the rights of the participants. So, for example, the sovereign states in the society of sovereign states may make use of their autonomous rights to discuss amongst themselves how world politics might be reorganized. Within the constraints of the anarchical society they might then set about bringing the changes decided upon into practice. They did this, for example, when they set up the United Nations Organization. However, they are limited in what changes can be considered. In terms of the ethical assumptions implicit in the practice, it would be unethical for some states to plot the takeover of other states without their consent. For example, it would be inappropriate for South Africa and Zimbabwe to engage in politics with a view to annexing Swaziland and Lesotho. The point being made here about what is involved in doing politics owes much to insights developed by Bernard Crick (Crick, 1964).

When we take stock of the anarchical practices within which we are constituted as free actors it becomes clear that there are many

---

31 The UN is something of an exception. Here the members of the anarchic system of sovereign states have formed together through a treaty an organization to which they have given the right to specify which actors are to be accorded the status of sovereign statehood in the SOSS.

good ethical reasons for supporting and nurturing them. In our normal day-to-day round in these practices, we seldom think of the good reasons for protecting these social wholes, because the very nature of anarchy requires the participants to be primarily concerned with self-defence and the pursuit of self-interest. As actors in these anarchies we (as individual civilians or as citizens within free states) are constituted to be primarily concerned with the preservation of ourselves as autonomous actors who are focused on the pursuit of our self-interests. It is this preoccupation with self that is the source of anarchy's strengths. In the normal course of events, through the participants' focus on self-defence and the pursuit of their own interests, the core values of these social practices as wholes are well protected. It is only in exceptional cases that this form of defence fails.

EVALUATING THE RIVAL READINGS OF PMCs

We are now in a position to evaluate the rival appraisals of PSCs and PMCs which we set out above. In the previous section we set out the global social practice within which the activities of PMCs and PSCs have to be understood. The practice within which they are located is global civil society (GCS). This, like the society of sovereign states (SOSS), is an anarchical society. The values realized in and through this practice include those of individual freedom and pluralism. Different people are free to use their individual rights to pursue different ideas of the good life. Furthermore, we have also seen that a reason for supporting this anarchical structure of rights holders is provided by the way in which it builds in a self-defence capacity without there having to be any central command structure. It builds in self-help as a component of the identity of the participants.

In the light of the above we can evaluate the rival appraisals of PMCs. First, consider the appraisal of those who portray PMCs as legitimate private companies satisfying a legitimate market demand. Are such appraisals supportive of the basic ethic underpinning the anarchical global civil society of rights holders? On the positive side of the balance sheet are the following considerations: In offering this interpretation these protagonists overtly indicate their support for the underlying ethic based on human rights. I have already indicated how the major companies all profess their support for human rights, the conventions set up to protect them and the many pieces of machinery in international law aimed at securing them. When asked about further regulation of their sector these companies have indicated that they are in favour of this.

Beyond these overt expressions of support for the underlying ethic of GCS, there are also structural reasons to believe that these companies will, indeed, do what they can to stay faithful to this creed. The argument here goes as follows. Because PMCs are private companies operating in a global market place, they are subject to competition from other players in this market. This provides them with a structural incentive to be true to their professed commitments. Were they to be shown to have failed, then, it is certain that other companies with better reputations would beat them in the next round of competition for contracts. The chief assets of these companies are their reputations. They are likely to work hard to preserve these. Scandals involving ethical impropriety would destroy their major asset.[32] Similarly, states that employ PMCs do not want to be shown to have hired companies that abuse human rights, so they have incentives to employ PMCs that are reputable.

On the negative side, this kind of assessment makes no mention of those many contracts that PMCs make with governments and with corporations that are secret and are nowhere made known to the public. That they do this type of thing is well known. Here there might well be a lack of openness which stretches from the tendering process that PMCs run in order to recruit subcontractors, through the execution phase of their projects and on to the monitoring of the contracts. Here, then, the background theory (extolling civil society's ability to promote freedom and diversity) provides us with a template against which we can examine the activities of PMCs. The secrecy here certainly does not seem to advance or protect these core values. By not mentioning this aspect of the subcontracting activities of PMCs, the assessment we are now considering may be considered deficient. Once again, as is so often the case, the deficiency is to be found in what their assessment hides or omits.

Another possible weakness in the appraisals of those defending PMCs arises from their lack of interest in exploring and discussing a

---

32 Scandals like that which arose in the Abu Ghraib prison in Iraq are devastating for PMCs.

number of difficult issues that might be interpreted as eroding the core values of the practice. One of these arises with regard to the ways in which PMCs regulate (or, more likely, fail to regulate) subcontractors. Is it possible to be sure that all subcontractors are good protectors of individual freedoms (human rights) and promoters of diversity?

In summary, then, the pro-PMC appraisals are in many ways supportive of the ethical philosophy internal to the practice of GCS. A main weakness of such appraisals lies in what is omitted, a failure fully to deal with the problem of secret relationships between PMCs and the services that they purchase and failing to deal with the problem of regulating subcontractors.

Next, let us consider the ethically negative appraisals of PMCs. These charge that PMCs are a threat to human rights. On this view, they pose a threat to human rights in a number of different ways: Such companies, it is said, are motivated by the profit motive and may cut corners to maximize profits rather than doing what is necessary to protect human rights; since the companies are private companies they are not responsible to democratically elected governments in the way that traditional military structures are; the internal structures of PMCs are not transparent and we cannot be sure that those who work for them will be subject to the same level of discipline that we can expect from traditional soldiers; such companies employ people from an international pool of labour – thus, states who employ PMCs will be making use of 'foreign' soldiers to do the military tasks usually reserved for national armies; and so on. Does this kind of appraisal uphold or undermine the practice of GCS within which the appraisers, and the rest of us, are constituted as rights holders? Does it accord with the embedded ethic of this institution with its focus on the preservation of individual freedoms and tolerance of diversity?

On the positive side, such appraisals endorse the value of human rights. The ethical wrongdoing which PMCs are likely to commit are all portrayed as involving the abuse of human rights. They expressly show concern for such rights. So this kind of appraisal does not undermine the core value produced by GCS.

Furthermore, the following set of arguments against PMCs show these appraisers to be endorsing prime GCS values. Their lack of transparency, their lack of accountability, their propensity to employ foreigners, their obsessive pursuit of profit are all said to threaten human rights in ways that would not come about if states continued to use their own military establishments rather than privatized ones. These points all reiterate and reinforce the core values of GCS, in that what is threatened by these characteristics are human rights. The typical recommendations which often follow such negative evaluations of PMCs usually call for a whole range of controls on PMCs including a requirement that they be licensed by national governments; that they be forced to comply with rigorously controlled training requirements for their employees and that they be subject to strict regulation by the states within which they are based. Such regulation ought to cover the tendering process, the recruitment process, the execution phase and the monitoring of all aspects of their activities. All of these controls ought to be put in place by the sovereign states within which they are based. In short, in these appraisals, the values constituted in global civil society are being endorsed, but the claim being made is that civilians cannot be trusted to deploy force in defence of these values. Civil society needs to be protected by a higher-order institution, the society of sovereign democratic states. The implied answer to the problems identified with PMCs is at every point that they ought to be dealt with by the governments of democratic states making use of their own citizens in state-run military institutions.

What such appraisals fail to confront is: Why should we believe that the use of a state-run military apparatus is less likely to abuse human rights in foreign places than privately-run military companies? After all, there is plenty of evidence that state military machines have proved quite capable of conducting gross human rights abuses, especially in times of war, both conventional wars and unconventional wars. Controlling such abuses becomes especially difficult when state-run military machines are operating far from the home state. What is particularly difficult to comprehend about the anti-PMC argument is just how and why those who propound it think states would provide the best defence of human rights in the international domain. Is it self-evident that the structural controls and the self-policing of PMCs in GCS is likely to be less effective in preventing human rights abuses than the controls administered by states – even democratic states. In particular, are sovereign states good at protecting human rights beyond their own borders?

This account of PMCs certainly does not fit with what the PMCs say about themselves, nor does it fit with what those who hire the services of PMCs say about what they are doing. The negative accounts of PMCs imply that those who produce positive assessments (this includes the PMCs themselves) are either duplicitous about what they are doing (pretending to be interested in upholding human rights while all the while knowing the PMCs are likely to harm them) or that they are not aware of just what the consequences of privatizing these functions are. To put it crudely, the implication is that those making positive assessments of PMCs are either dishonest or stupid.

GLOBAL CIVIL SOCIETY: A RECAPITULATION

The discussion above was not intended as an exhaustive account of private security companies and private military companies. The aim was to use the debate about these to bring to light key features of that social practice that I have called global civil society (GCS) and to highlight the ethics that underpin it. It is this practice that provides the framework within which the debate about PMCs is possible. In this section GCS has been shown to be a practice distinct from the practice of sovereign states. We, together with all those who participate in the debate about PSCs and PMCs, are only able to understand one another when we comprehend the wider social practice within which we are constituted as actors of a certain kind. This is global civil society – the society of rights holders. We have seen that the primary characteristics of this society are that it is borderless, that it is anarchical in form and that in it participants are constituted as holders of equal sets of fundamental human rights. In the normal pattern of conduct, participants in GCS use their rights in straightforward ways that do not pose to them any particular ethical problems. In this global society they buy and sell goods and services, they set up companies, they establish friendships, they go on tours, they attend educational institutions, find romantic partners and so on. In their day-to-day acts the participants adhere to the ethical constraints, implicit in the practice, without difficulty and without consciously considering the ethical dimensions of what they are doing. However, from time to time rights holders confront explicit ethical problems. The emergence of PSCs and PMCs has presented participants, that is, all of us, with several such problems. Here we cannot but get involved in a process of interaction in which we have to appraise the phenomena that confront us, in all their ethical complexity, prior to deciding what to do. In making these appraisals we engage in a back-and-forth process of argument in which we seek either to support or undermine the ethical standing of our interlocutors who propose alternative understandings of the practice. It is through this process of ethical argument that we construct and reconstruct the social practices within which international relations are conducted.

In the preceding discussion we saw how, in the debate about PMCs, one side of the conversation seeks to portray PMCs as upholding the core values of GCS, whereas the other side seeks to erode the standing of PSCs and PMCs and those who serve in them by showing how they undermine precisely the same core values, portraying them as little better than gangs of mercenaries with all the negative ethical connotations that that term holds. It is important to stress, once again, that these claims and counterclaims are not peripheral to what is happening in Iraq at the moment. These are not mere ethical niceties being discussed by philosophers in ivory towers but are the essential interpretive engagements that have to be made by any participant in the unfolding drama. Participation requires analysis. Those who interpret the activities of Erinsys, Blackwater, ArmorGroup, Halliburton (and many others) as agents supportive of global civil society will act in one way, whereas those who see these companies as threats to human rights will act entirely differently. The dispute between the two sides is not an empirical one; it cannot be settled by observation alone, but requires those involved in it to engage in a profound way with some complex ethical arguments.

At the end of our discussion of PSCs and PMCs it became clear that those who portrayed them in an ethically negative light did so by linking GCS to the ethical values embedded in the society of sovereign states. They presented us with a negative picture of civil society such that its problems could only be solved by sovereign democratic states. What we see happening here, then, is that the PMCs located in civil society are being ethically evaluated from the point of view of the society of sovereign states. The ethical evaluation becomes more complex as the two practices, GCS and the society of sovereign states, are shown to be linked in ethically significant ways. To enrich our understanding of contemporary international relations we now need to turn to a more detailed consideration of the relationship between global civil society (GCS) and the society of sovereign states. We need to investigate the configuration of this double anarchy.

3

ETHICAL INCOHERENCE: INDIVIDUAL RIGHTS *VERSUS* STATES' RIGHTS

Almost everyone worldwide is simultaneously constituted as a participant in global civil society (GCS) and also as a participant in the society of sovereign states (SOSS). In the former they hold the status of civilians, the possessors of sets of fundamental first-generation human rights; in the latter they are constituted as citizens in sovereign states. That they are participants in both has produced for them a number of what often appear to be intractable problems. Engagement with these problems is at the very heart of contemporary international politics. A failure to understand this set of problems will result in an overall failure to understand contemporary international relations. Let us examine this more closely.

One possible (and seemingly very strong) assessment of contemporary international relations suggests that we face a fundamental ethical choice: Are we to live our lives committed to the achievement and upholding of individual human rights for all people everywhere, that is, are we to uphold and improve global civil society? Or, conversely, is our primary commitment to the upholding and protecting of the system of sovereign states within which we enjoy our citizenship rights? There are a range of issue areas in contemporary international relations which seem to put this choice to us. Consider some illustrative examples.

A stark form of this choice appears to arise when we consider the case of international migrants, be they asylum seekers, refugees or economic migrants. In terms of the ethical tenets imposed on us by our membership of GCS, all people everywhere have the same fundamental set of first-generation human rights. These include the standard personal rights such as the right not to be killed, assaulted, tortured; the right to freedom of contract, the right to freedom of assembly, to freedom of movement, to freedom of speech, the right to own property and the right to freedom of conscience.[1] Migrants, of course, being humans, also have these human rights. When migrants, making use of their right to freedom of movement, arrive here, when they move into the states within which we live, they are often presented as posing a threat to the interests of our sovereign states and to our rights and interests as citizens in such states. As citizens we talk of migrants threatening 'our jobs' or threatening 'our national identity' and 'our culture'. Here, then, it appears that we have to choose whether to uphold our civil society commitments to fundamental human rights or whether to uphold the citizenship rights we enjoy in the society of sovereign states. Conflict assessed in this way has manifested itself in any number of states recently, including Britain, France, Italy, Spain, South Africa, Chad, Australia and the USA to mention but a few. On the basis of such assessments many governments pass legislation to prevent the arrival of such migrants and to secure the repatriation of those who have already arrived. Yet, the migrants remain a problem and the problem is not merely the technical one of how to keep them out (through higher fences, more border guards, wider buffer strips and so on). If it were simply a technical problem, finding the solution could be left to engineers. They could be given increased budgets to find better ways and means of keeping the unwanted migrants out. Such people cannot be treated in this way because the problem here is not merely one of controlling the bodies of migrants as physical objects but is also (and more importantly) understood to be an ethical problem. These migrants are not just moving bodies to be stopped, steered or destroyed, but are humans with whom we know ourselves to be in

1 There are ongoing arguments among civilians about what the complete list of rights should include, but there is agreement about a core of first-generation rights.

some kind of ethical relationship.[2] Once it is acknowledged that the problem has to be thought through in ethical terms, then it appears that we face the stark ethical choice: prioritize the right of states to curtail migration as they see fit or prioritize individual rights, which would place severe limits on the right of states to bar migrants entry.

The same issue crops up when we consider macro-economic policy on a global scale. Here, according to one account, it would appear that those favouring individual human rights would support the opening up of international markets to the free flow of the factors of production including, of course, labour. Whereas those who take the sovereign state within the society of sovereignty states to have ethical primacy would not demur at the introduction of protectionist policies. Here again it appears as if we are presented with a fundamental ethical choice that would inform how we understand migrancy in all its forms.

Another issue area within which this seeming clash between global civil society and the system of sovereign states comes to light is with regard to humanitarian intervention. Since the end of the Cold War it has become possible for strong states to consider intervening in the internal affairs of weaker states in order to protect human rights. Several high-profile interventions have taken place in places such as the former Yugoslavia, Somalia and Sierra Leone. In such cases, it would appear that we all, as participants in the two major global practices, have to choose between upholding the right of states to non-intervention or upholding individual human rights. Interventionists maintain that wherever human rights violations are taking place, and where all other means of intervention to prevent them have been tried, then a case can be made for forceful intervention to protect these basic human rights. State-centric theorists advise that priority ought to be given to the maintenance of state sovereignty – this requires non-intervention.[3]

2 Proof of this ethical concern is to be found in the *1951 Geneva Convention Relating to the Status of Refugees* (and the subsequent Protocols) which is accepted by a vast majority of states worldwide.

3 This latter position is vigorously defended by the states of the so-called 'Global South'. Their commitment to the preservation of sovereign statehood is extremely strong. Witness the general reaction of African states to the human rights' abuses taking place in Zimbabwe over recent years. They have been resolutely opposed to external intervention into the internal affairs of Zimbabwe.

A further set of examples that appear to present us with a plain choice between individual rights and states' rights emerges when we consider disputes that have arisen over a number of cultural practices such as strong forms of patriarchy and the practice of female genital mutilation. Here again it seems as if we face a choice between protecting human rights and upholding the fundamental rights of sovereign states to promote whatever cultural practices they deem fit for protection.[4]

The tensions discussed above have led to a highly sophisticated discussion in the discipline of IR in what has come to be known as the 'cosmopolitan/communitarian' debate (Buchanan, 1989; Cochran, 1995; Mulhall & Swift, 1992; Linklater, 1990; Etzioni, 1998). The cosmopolitans assert the primacy of individual rights and the communitarians stress the importance of the rights of political communities. The primary political community is customarily taken to be the nation state.

An implication of this line of reasoning is that, when we as individuals confront this kind of choice, a choice between sticking with our commitments to a scheme of universal human rights for everyone within a global civil society or staying with our commitment to our fellow citizens within the society of sovereign states, then we stand before a classical tragic choice.[5] We find ourselves in the typical 'lose-lose' predicament of tragedy.[6] The choice before us appears to be tragic because whatever course of action we undertake will result in us having to renege on a set of values that is of defining value for

---

4 For a discussion of the role of culture in understanding international relations see Lapid & Kratochwil, 1996, Introduction.

5 On the inevitability of tragedy in international politics see Lebow, 2003, Schmidt, 2004, Spirtas, 1996.

6 In the Greek tragic plays the hero is presented to the audience as standing before an *agon* where requiring a choice between two ethical imperatives both of which are ethically fundamental for him. Whatever one he or she chooses will result in him or her falling foul of the alternative imperative not followed. Thus, Antigone has to choose whether to obey the ethical imperative of family life that she retrieve her brother's body from outside the walls of the city in order to bring it home for a proper burial or to obey the political/ethical imperative that she obey her King who commands that she leave the body there outside the walls as an example to others who would defy his authority. She finds herself in the typical ethical lose/lose predicament of tragedy.

us.[7] Thus, to use yet another example, if we choose to support protectionist economic policies, then we are letting down our commitment to millions of other rights holders in GCS who are entitled to participate in that part of the market straddled by our state. Were we to choose to favour the rights of our sovereign state rather than the rights of individuals in GCS, then there is a very real sense that by doing such a thing we would be renouncing our right to be considered bona fide members of the rights-respecting practice, global civil society. We would be indicating to all who would notice that our membership of GCS was hypocritical. We could only be taken to be committed to the practice of universal human rights insofar as participating in that practice did not involve us doing anything counter to what was required of us as participants in the society of sovereign states. The contrary would also apply. Were we to choose to act in accordance with the dictates of GCS, then we would have to be understood as hypocritical members of the community of sovereign states. Our predicament in such cases, then, appears to be tragic in the strongest sense of the word. We set out to be ethical actors, but, by acting in terms of one set of our ethical commitments, we undercut another set of ethical commitments. By doing the correct ethical thing in one practice, we end up committing an ethical wrong in another.

A good example of such a tragic choice appears to arise with regard to the complex problem of humanitarian intervention in the domestic affairs of sovereign states other than our own. If our fundamental commitment is to human rights then we should consistently favour such intervention in the appropriate cases, but this might involve us not respecting the sovereignty of the states being intervened in. Doing this might throw doubt on the sincerity of our membership of the community of sovereign states. Whatever we do in the face of these dilemmas we are going to be forced into hypocrisy and tragedy. Consider another example presented by the case of an Australian citizen who is concerned about the plight of the boat people seeking asylum in Australia. A concerned citizen who is also at the same time a civilian in global civil society might be concerned about the threat posed to the rights of these people were they to be returned to their country of origin. Irrespective of Australia's

7 This line of thinking informs the writing of John Mearsheimer (Mearsheimer, 2001).

international treaty commitments, this person might consider that such 'boat people' have a full set of human rights and are thus entitled to use their right of freedom of movement to move to Australia. This line of thinking would apply no matter how many people approached the shores of Australia. As a civilian this person should endeavour to respect such people's rights. However, as a citizen he or she might be worried about the impact of such an influx on the Australian polity. He might decide with a mild sense of tragedy that in this case his interests as an Australian override his global interests as a civilian. From his individual point of view it may seem as if there is no way of reconciling the conflict. It is a hard choice that simply has to be made in a less than ideal world. This, it might be thought, is the way of the world. Tragic choices cannot be avoided.

The tension we have been discussing also underlies the ongoing and often acrimonious discussion about the merits of globalization. Those who speak in favour of globalization often build their case on a strong defence of a global liberal economic order. The ethical argument in support of this is one or another version of the cosmopolitan argument. Oversimplifying greatly, the case for globalization usually includes all or some of the following arguments. The main feature of globalization is the spread of the global capitalist market. A primary feature of this market is that it consists of private rights holders who buy and sell goods and services in a global market place. The actors are guided primarily by market considerations (primarily the pursuit of profit) and not by concern for the interests of the sovereign states within which they are located. The actors' interests are private interests and not national ones. The increased scale of the global market has resulted in an increased product. Through a trickle-down effect this is working to the long-term benefit of everyone. Through their pursuit of self-interest private actors thus unintentionally bring about a public good, the growth of capital. This can be reinvested for further growth and it can be taxed by governments to provide a 'safety net' of benefits for those who cannot manage the competition. The social scientific theories about how precisely the market works are complicated and contentious, but these are not of concern here. The central point here is that those who make the case for market-driven globalization have clearly chosen global civil society as the practice which is of more importance than the other global practice, the society of states. While not denying the importance of states, these theorists stress that the role of states must be a limited one that leaves maximum space open for individual rights holders to arrange their own lives as they see fit. On this view the state ought to serve the market (Stopford & Strange, 1991, Chapter 13).

The pro-globalization argument we have outlined above is an ethical one (asserting that it is wrong for states to curb rights holders exercising their rights). It is also empirical (claiming that a consequence of obeying this ethical imperative will be to bring about material results that work to the benefit of all rights holders)[8] and it also makes predictions about the way things will develop in future (claiming that the market will triumph in the long run, even against states that attempt to oppose it). At base, though, the liberal argument rests on a cosmopolitan ethic according to which there exists a worldwide society of rights holders whose rights ought not to be infringed by states or any other institutional actors.

A converse position is taken by those who argue against globalization. Here, too, there is an underlying ethical position, but in this case it is a communitarian one. According to those who argue from this point of view, priority is to be given to the system of sovereign states for each state embodies and represents an ethical community usually referred to as the nation.[9] Membership of such a primary ethical community is of fundamental importance to all people everywhere. From an ethical point of view what matters is the political community which is the ethical home for each one of us. Some version of this argument is to be found in realist understandings of international relations, pluralist accounts and all those accounts which stress the primacy of nations and national self-determination. According to this view the process of globalization (which is powered by the expansion of the global capitalist economic order) is a major threat to the values embedded in the system of sovereign states. Globalization threatens the autonomy of states and thus threatens the autonomy of individual political communities. Those who seek to promote the cause of global civil society (and *a fortiori* human rights) are, on this view, to be understood as undermining the autonomy of our fundamental political communities. A

8 Or at least work more to their benefit than any feasible alternative arrangement.
9 See the discussion of this issue in: Michael Walzer (Walzer, 1980).

more complex version of this argument has it that, under the guise of promoting cosmopolitan values, certain states, the USA and other advanced industrial states, are in fact furthering their national interests. This is an ethical wrong that ought to be opposed for it amounts to nothing much more than a form of imperialism by those states that have been made strong by their position in the capitalist market.

In sum, then, the dispute between those who extol the virtues of globalization and those who oppose it can easily be construed as a version of the ethical dispute between cosmopolitans and communitarians.[10] On this assessment, it seems that once again we stand before an ethical choice – the rights of individual men and women in global civil society or the rights of citizens in sovereign states.

Is this evaluation of our current international order correct? Has the evolution of our international practices reached a point where we have to choose between pursuing individual human rights in a global civil society or promoting states' rights within a system of sovereign states? Although it often seems to us that we have to make just such a choice, in what follows I shall argue that this assessment is wrong. To understand our ethical position in the world in this way is to misunderstand it. Furthermore, to promote such a misunderstanding is to do something that is ethically wrong. The apparent choice arises only because the problem has been wrongly framed. Constitutive theory provides us with a better way of accounting for the apparent tensions between rights and sovereignty set out above.

RIGHTS AND SOVEREIGNTY: REFRAMING THE TENSION

Do we have to choose between human rights and states rights, between cosmopolitanism and communitarianism? Are the ethical commitments and bonds that we enjoy as civilians in global civil society completely at odds with the commitments and bonds that we have as citizens within the society of sovereign states? Is the practice of rights holders in global civil society in direct conflict with the practice of sovereign states such that we cannot coherently participate

10 For a clear setting out of contemporary understandings of international ethics in terms of the cosmopolitan communitarian debate see Brown, 1992, Introduction.

in both at once? The argument of this book is that the answer to all these questions is negative.

The flaw in the assessment under scrutiny is that it fails to take seriously the way in which we are constituted as free individuals through our simultaneous participation in both anarchical practices. The way in which the questions are framed suggests that we are in some sense external to these practices and are free to decide to which one we wish to commit. This way of framing the issue is wrong for we are not outsiders to these social practices, but insiders. We are constituted as the actors we are through our simultaneous participation in both global practices. It is wrong to conceive of ourselves as standing external to these anarchical societies wondering which to join, in the way that we might contemplate joining this or that social club. What we need to understand is that our relationship to these practices is an internal one. In them we are constituted, through elaborate systems of reciprocal recognition, as who we value ourselves to be. Furthermore, our identities as who we value ourselves to be depend on the maintenance of a sophisticated relationship of interdependence between the two global practices. Constitutive theory suggests that the relationship between the two practices is a sophisticated one such that certain ethical shortcomings we experience in the one are remedied through our simultaneous participation in the other. In short, as things currently stand, we are both civilians and citizens. Furthermore, we value the ethical standing that we enjoy in these roles. Let us examine how it is possible coherently and simultaneously to maintain standing as civilian and citizen – how it is possible to participate in GCS and the SOSS at once without the attempt leading to tragedy.

What we shall see is that there is a way of understanding global civil society and the society of sovereign states that shows them to be complementary practices – that shows how the latter overcomes ethical shortcomings experienced in the former. Crucially, however, we shall see that the problems are overcome not by replacing civil society with the society of states but by supplementing the former with the latter.

In global civil society rights holders (all of us) hold the first-generation rights of civilians. These are negative liberties situated in an anarchical structure. Through possession of these liberties rights holders are able to construct for themselves lives in which they pursue very different notions of the good. Yet, although civilians are constituted as free in this society, there are a number of significant ethical shortcomings that become manifest over time. First, civilians are in a state of permanent competition with one another for a range of scarce things, such as wealth, position and territory. This competitive feature of GCS leads civilians to suffer feelings of alienation from their fellows. Furthermore, although civilians have rights to make contracts with other civilians, not all of them (not all of us) make good use of their rights. Some will be more successful than others in the contracts they make. This might be as a result of simple luck, being in the right place at the right time or being born with certain key talents necessary for success. Over time some will build on their success to accumulate capital of various kinds, such as social capital, financial capital, educational capital and so on. Civilians will pass this capital on to their offspring down the generations. With time, but not through any wrongdoing by rights holders, the anarchical society will turn (and has turned) into an unequal society. The society will divide into classes, the haves and the have-nots. These inequalities will not necessarily stand in any close relationship to desert. In sum, civil society, without wrongdoing on the part of particular civilians, will facilitate and produce ethically noxious outcomes such as endemic competition, alienation and inequality of power and resources. We may see these as injustices.[11] To summarize, in GCS, then, some good things are achieved; participants are constituted as free in an arrangement that promotes diversity. But these are countered by the ethical shortcomings mentioned.

These problems are to some measure solved in the contemporary world in the society of sovereign states.[12] For civilians (all of us) are not only civilians but are also citizens within sovereign states in the society of such states. As such they (we) gain an additional ethical status. Citizens have a set of rights which, in part at least, remedy the

11 It is worth mentioning that some theorists, like Robert Nozick, who built on the work of John Locke, argued that there is nothing unjust about inequality that emerges in this way (Nozick, 1974; Locke, 1952).

12 The insights here are very loosely derived from the political philosophy of G. W. F. Hegel. See especially Hegel, 1973. Hegel's theory is highly complex and rests on an argument about the progressive development of *geist* in the world. I have attempted to extract insights from his approach, but without immersing myself (or the reader) in any complex metaphysics.

shortcomings experienced in civil society. Where civilians are in competition with one another, citizens are united as members of equal worth in the state within which they enjoy this status. The alienation experienced in civil society is overcome through common membership of a sovereign state that itself enjoys the recognition of other states. Sovereign states have governments which can, through deliberate action, remedy some of the problems encountered in civil society. The government can do things to alleviate the endemic competition, the alienation and the inequalities brought about through the operation of civil society over time. Governments may do this within the territories of their own states, but they can also, acting jointly, achieve a similar result in the international domain by creating international institutions such as the EU and the WTO and also through the delivery of aid and through the mechanisms of international financial institutions such as the IMF and the World Bank.

Let us examine more closely how states might overcome the ethical shortcomings of civil society. First, they engender a feeling of togetherness and fraternity amongst citizens. This identity is constructed through the use of patriotic or nationalistic language. Such discourses construct amongst citizens a feeling of a 'we' who together confront 'others' who might be enemies or at least competitor states. In their citizenship role people no longer only confront one another in ceaseless market-based competition but are united in pursuit of what they have in common, the national interest. Second, the structural inequalities that are endemic to civil society can be counteracted by the policies and actions of state governments. Through systems of taxation governments are able to overcome some of the unequal distributions that arise through the normal working of civil society. The inequalities generated by civil society can be remedied by the state which provides a whole range of services for its citizens. Third, where the sovereign states are democratic states, these effects can be brought about with the participation and consent of the citizens concerned.[13]

Crucially, the results spelled out in the previous paragraph can be

---

13 Note that Hegel did not consider the ethical advances posed by the advent of democracy within states. At the time he was writing in the early 19th century, the widespread advance of democratic forms of government within states had not yet taken place.

achieved without dismantling civil society. In the contemporary world all states do (with greater or lesser success) the things mentioned in the previous paragraph, but, for the most part, in doing them they are careful not to destroy civil society. In particular, they are careful to nurture that portion of civil society that we know as the market.

Let us illustrate the account given above about how citizenship repairs some of the ethical shortcomings experience by civilians by considering how this might play out in the life of a single individual. Consider the hypothetical case of Sipho Khumalo, a civilian in global civil society who lives in South Africa. As a civilian he considers himself to have a full set of first-generation fundamental human rights. He recognizes his fellow participants in civil society wherever they happen to be in the world as having an equal set of such rights. In this role as civilian, he vigorously pursues his own interests and his own understanding of the good (which in his case, let us say, is a Christian one). He understands that his fellow civilians have a right to do the same. Wherever he goes in the world he considers himself to be a rights holder, free to make contracts with, for example, Japanese business people, free to strike up friendships with people he meets while in France, free to join in prayer with fellow believers he comes across in Ethiopia, free to pursue a romance with someone he meets in Italy. In all this he knows that others might be competing with him for business, friends, worshippers and lovers. Yet, in spite of his ethical right to these benefits, Sipho experiences the ethical problems of civil society: He is tired and suffers anxiety as a result of the ongoing competition; he feels alienated from his co-workers and from many neighbours; over time he notes that some civilians are clearly doing better than he is. He notices the emergence of great inequalities of wealth, status and power. The distribution of the good things in life is skewed in favour of the fortunate few.

Concurrent with his activities as a civilian in global civil society, though, Sipho is a citizen of the Republic of South Africa, which is a democracy in the system of sovereign states. As such he knows himself to be of equal status with his fellow citizens; he knows he has equal rights to stand for government, participate in elections and to enjoy the benefits of legislation passed by his government. He knows that much government activity is directed towards redistribution aimed at rectifying some of the inequalities brought about in civil society. Whereas, in his role as civilian he feels himself to be in competition with other civilians living in South Africa, in his role as citizen he knows himself to be in a fraternal relationship with them such that they have a common interest in the success of the South African state. What is important to note here is that the state recognizes the importance of civil society and seeks to allow the good ethical outcomes mentioned without, in the process, destroying civil society and the individual rights created within it.

On the assessment of the contemporary world offered by constitutive theory, what individuals value, then, are their civilian rights enjoyed in global civil society *and* their citizenship rights enjoyed in sovereign states. The practices are not rivals, but must be understood as complementing one another. The way in which the two practices are made to cohere is through the provision that states must respect the civilian rights people enjoy in GCS.

For any reader who doubts what I have claimed above, there is ample evidence that those who participate in global civil society and also in the system of sovereign states value their simultaneous participation in both. First, most states belong to the UN.[14] The UN as an institution is committed to the promotion and protection of human rights worldwide. From this it follows that states and the citizens that comprise them do not see a commitment to human rights *per se* as a threat to their sovereignty. Second, the UN as an international organization is committed to the promotion of democracy among its member states. The idea of democracy is closely associated with ideas of individual human rights. So, here again, it is clear that the society of sovereign states does not declare itself against human rights, respect for which is the defining feature of global civil society. Third, all the citizens in all the states (within the system of states) are participants in the global capitalist market. A defining feature of this market is that it is based on notions of individual rights (to property, to contract, to association etc). So, here again, we can see that the participants in the society of sovereign states are not hostile to the reality of participating in GCS. Fourth, most states that have come into being over the last quarter of a century have adopted constitutions that commit them to the

14 Of the 193 sovereign states, 192 are members of the United Nations Organization.

protection of human rights through Bills of Rights and through their legal systems. Fifth, and finally, if we look at what civilians in global civil society say, we do not find that they are in general opposed to citizenship in sovereign states. Quite the contrary, in general, civilians look to their states to protect and nurture the human rights that they consider themselves to have in global civil society. The state (within the society of such states) and the citizenship that they enjoy in it is seen as supportive of human rights. Indeed, it is the major institution available for the protection of human rights. This is not to deny that there are many individual states that, far from protecting the civilian rights of their citizens, are in fact a threat to them (North Korea would be a good example).

From the above we can conclude that, in general, the individuals who are at one and the same time participants in civil society and in the society of states do not understand the roles of civilian and citizen to conflict with one another. The way in which conflict is avoided is through the adoption of the rule that sovereign states ought to nurture and protect individual human rights.

Although we gain added ethical standing through our participation in sovereign states within the system of sovereign states, it is also the case that states are useful to us in an instrumental way when it comes to protecting human rights. The liberal tradition in ethical theory has always defended states as mechanisms rights holders have established for the protection of their pre-existing human rights. As Nozick put it, states are protection associations that rights holders pay to protect their fundamental rights. In many cases this is indeed true. It is often the case that the institutional machinery available to states does provide a good protection for the rights of civilians. There are many states, though, where corrupt government bodies in fact threaten rights rather than protect them. Constitutive theory as set out here, while admitting that states might well be good mechanisms for the protection of rights, also asserts that states have an another important ethical (as opposed to instrumental) role. This is that in the society of sovereign states people gain an important ethical status, that of citizen.

In the light of the above, what are we to say about the apparent tensions between rights and sovereignty that we have alluded to above? Are these fictions or illusions? Is there nothing real about them? The answer, I would suggest, is that these tensions must be read, not as indicating an *overall* incompatibility between the practices within which civilianship and citizenship are made possible, not as indicating the necessity of a choice between the two, but as indicating *specific* internal tensions within the combined institutional structure of GCS and the society of sovereign states. Instead of portraying us as standing before a radical choice, a better assessment is that the problem of migrants, the problem of humanitarian intervention and the problems associated with the expansion of global civil society (often referred to as the process of globalization) present us with specific ethico/institutional problems – problems that require of us that we consider what modifications of this edifice, this double anarchy, are called for in order to resolve the tensions. The questions for us are: As participants in this double anarchy, what transformations, modifications and adjustments are called for in order to resolve the tensions mentioned? How can we modify the practices to alleviate the tensions, without at the same time destroying those valued ethical statuses we enjoy within them?

Following the procedures developed earlier in this book, in order to find answers to these questions we need to make use of the supporting ethic underpinning this practice of practices – this double anarchy.

THE ETHICAL UNDERPINNING OF DOUBLE ANARCHY

As has been set out above, the global practices within which we are constituted as international actors are global civil society (GCS) and the society of sovereign states (SOSS) understood as complementary social institutions. The system of sovereign states within which we enjoy citizenship rights builds on the ethical identities made possible within global civil society within which actors are established as civilians – as individual rights holders. The two taken together form a practice of practices, the double anarchy. Following the sequence of argument that went before, we may now ask: What is the supporting ethical theory which underpins the double anarchy seen as a whole? What, from an ethical point of view, is to be said in favour of this double anarchy? What ethical values does it make possible?

The answers are straightforward and follow from what went before in our discussion of global civil society and the society of sovereign states. Earlier we established that the prime values made possible within these global social practices are freedom and diversity.[15] In global civil society participants are constituted as rights holders, as the holders of specific sets of freedoms. These freedoms make it possible for the participants to pursue a great diversity of life plans built on different ideas of the good. In the society of sovereign states, the participants are constituted as citizens within sovereign free states. Each state is granted freedom subject to the limitation that it respect the freedom of other states. Within the domain of freedom accorded to it, each state is free to pursue its own concept of the good. Here again (as in GCS) the practice creates free actors and encourages diversity. It creates the conditions of possibility for diversity to emerge.

Once the two practices are linked, as has happened in the contemporary world, with the result that most people are simultaneously participants in both, then the supporting philosophy of each remains intact. However, for this to be possible, without plunging the participants into contradictions, the participants have to accept a common rule which is that as citizens in the system of sovereign states they have to respect the civilian rights that they and others enjoy in GCS. This is an obvious step once we acknowledge that the system of sovereign states is to be understood as building on and improving the moral standing that the participants of global civil society enjoy. It follows then that each sovereign state is to be understood as being located on a specific portion of global civil society and that each state is primarily responsible for the protection of that portion of GCS. It is required to protect the civilian rights of the people that live there; however, it is also required to respect the civilian rights of people wherever they happen to be.

What is crucial for a full understanding of the supporting ethical philosophy here is that it must be understood as underpinning the structure of the double anarchy as a whole. As a social whole that spans the globe the two anarchies combine to create two types of freedom and to promote diversity for actors in two different roles, as civilians and as citizens. What is created then is freedom for individuals in civil society and freedom for individuals in free states, and

---

15 It would be difficult, difficult in logic, for a person claiming civilian and citizenship rights for him- or herself, to deny that these values underpinned the practices.

also diversity amongst individuals in civil society and diversity amongst states within the society of states.

Where ethical tensions arise (where hard cases occur) within this double anarchy, it is to this supporting philosophy that we should turn for guidance. When evaluating rival assessments, with their associated policy prescriptions, we ought to turn to this supportive ethical theory to help us evaluate the assessments prior to deciding what to do. We shall consider some practical examples of how this might be done, but first I wish to make some general points about what is involved in dealing with internal ethical tensions in a two-tiered anarchy.

ETHICAL TRANSFORMATION IN A DOUBLE ANARCHY

I have presented an account of contemporary international life that portrays it as a practice of practices that consists of two complementary anarchies. The definitional feature of an anarchical social formation is that its organizational form is flat and not hierarchical. In it, all the actors are considered to be equal and on the same plane. In anarchies the participants are constituted as free in specified domains. Finally, in anarchies there is no central rule-making authority – there is no central government. From all of this it follows that, where ethical tensions arise within an anarchy or between one anarchy and another associated with it, it is not possible to hand the matter over for resolution to some governmental body, for there is no such thing. Whatever rule changes are called for to resolve the ethical tensions that emerge, they will have to be identified, discussed and introduced into everyday practice by the participants themselves. Such changes will only come about through a complex *political* process. The diverse participants with their many different ideas of the good will have to go through a process of discussion (probably a long one) in order to identify what the tensions are and how they might be resolved. The key point is that anarchies can only be transformed through politics. However, the political process required to modify these practices in order to deal with the tensions mentioned will itself endorse, make manifest and strengthen the very freedoms that are constituted within them. In the political process aimed at resolving ethical hard cases, the participants will reassert their equality as free actors within both GCS and society of states. In these practices, as we have seen, all individual civilians and all individual sovereign states are entitled to an equal voice in the political process. They are entitled to this by the constitutive rules of both practices. These rules give ethical power and influence to actors that, from a material and military perspective, are weak. The constitutive rules delegitimize attempts by the strong to impose any form of plutocracy on the smaller and weaker participants. Some states might attempt this kind of imposition, but in so doing they will lay themselves open to criticism from their fellow participants in terms of the fundamental constitutive rules of the society of states.

Let us call the process of resolving ethical tensions in the double anarchy a process of ethical adjustment. As already indicated, because there is no central government, adjustments in anarchical societies cannot be imposed from the centre onto the whole. Whatever rule changes take place will do so in a way that is quite unlike the process of legislation that takes place within states. Such changes must necessarily take place in a piecemeal way. New rules will have to be accepted and adopted by the participants. In some areas of the anarchical societies this might happen quickly, whereas in other areas it may take a long time. The pace of transformation will be asymmetrical. Furthermore, there is a real sense in which the process of adjustment can only proceed through a process of consent by the participants. From this we can conclude that transformation will often be slow. Finally, because the process of adjustment is asymmetrical between different areas, there is likely to be a great deal of experimentation in the different parts of the two anarchies. This will afford the participants the chance to see how different modifications turn out before committing themselves to following suit.

In the light of the above, what are we to make of the tensions between individual rights and state sovereignty that we outlined above. Are these illusory? How ought we to think of the problem of migrants, the problem of humanitarian intervention, the problem of globalization and so on.[16] What are we to make of the assessments that picture us facing a choice between the practices?

16 Further questions in this vein include: Does the creation of the International Criminal Court threaten the sovereign status of states? Do interventionist peace-keeping operations delivered by the United Nations Security Council pose a threat to the autonomy of states?

As indicated earlier, constitutive theory suggests that assessments which portray us as standing at a crucial crossroad in world affairs are wide of the mark. The flaw in such assessments is, as is so often the case, one of omission. Those that stress the importance of free markets above the rights of states are guilty of omitting to indicate the ethical importance of our being constituted as citizens in free states. Similarly, those evaluations that stress the importance of sovereign autonomy for states omit the importance for individuals that they be rights holders in global civil society. Constitutive theory's primary strength is that it offers a holist analysis of international affairs that is not guilty of such standard omissions.

In what follows I shall demonstrate the application of constitutive theory to a range of contemporary problems that confront us in contemporary international affairs. I shall use the method to analyse the problems associated with migrants, humanitarian intervention, globalization, torture as an international issue and global terrorism.

MIGRANTS IN WORLD POLITICS

On the assessment considered above it would seem that migrants present us with a clear example of the ethical choice that we are considering: prefer the rights of individuals or prefer the rights of states. Is this account of how things stand in international relations today correct?

Constitutive theory offers us an alternative assessment of the phenomenon of illegal migrancy in the contemporary world – one that coheres better with what we say about ourselves and the social arrangements within which we live. It offers us a way of interpreting this phenomenon that takes seriously both individual civilian rights and the rights of sovereign states.

Constitutive theory starts from the analysis outlined above which argued that the best supporting theory for the double anarchy of contemporary world politics is one which shows how it creates the conditions of possibility of freedom and diversity for individual men and women and for sovereign states. With this supporting theory in mind we can now ask: How are we to understand illegal migrancy?

In terms of constitutive theory we are to understand that, as things presently stand, we are already in an ethical relationship to all the other participants in the only two global practices of our time,

GCS and society of sovereign states. Migrants are not perfect strangers, but are our co-participants in the double anarchy. We constitute one another as free through recognizing one another as civilians in civil society and as citizens in the society of sovereign states. Migrants are not to be understood as outsiders with whom at some future stage we (whoever 'we' might happen to be) might forge ethical relationships. Any set of migrants, be they asylum seekers, refugees or economic migrants, are all to be understood from the outset as being, together with us, both civilians and citizens.

In order to give a satisfactory account of an influx of illegal migrants from, let us say, Zimbabwe into South Africa, constitutive theory directs us to ask: How are we to interpret these actions given that the actors are all civilians and citizens and may be taken as committed to the core values of the double anarchy (global civil society and the society of sovereign states)? We know that for the people involved, in the normal course of events, *illegal* migration is not ethical. There are well-known laws and regulations governing the movement of people between states. These include legal procedures to be adhered to requiring appropriate travel documents such as passports, health inoculation certificates, visas and work-permits. For the most part these are adhered to by tourists, business people, students, religious pilgrims, migrant workers and so on. People who contravene such laws and regulations are deemed to have behaved not only illegally but also unethically. Smuggling oneself (or other people) across international borders is deemed a criminal activity. But are such interpretations always right? Or are there circumstances where illegal migration ought to be understood as ethically justifiable action? The argument to be presented here is that there are, indeed, such cases. There are times when acting illegally is the ethically right thing to do. Let us examine some of them.

In terms of the ethic embedded in the double anarchy, states are required to respect and protect the rights of civilians in their territories. For the most part states do this. But in some cases, far from protecting civilian rights, the governments of states come to threaten them. The recent history of the government of Zimbabwe headed by President Robert Mugabe provides a good example of this. In that country the government has abused the civilian rights of many Zimbabweans. It has curbed their freedom of speech, their freedom of association, their freedom of the press, their right to academic freedom, their rights to *habeas corpus*, their rights to safety of the person, their right not to be assaulted, tortured or killed. There can be little doubt that the Zimbabwean government, with all the power at its disposal, is an active and ongoing threat to civilians in that country and, in particular, to those who oppose the government. Many of them have fled to South Africa and to other neighbouring states. For such people their opportunities to obtain the right travel documents are limited, both because the Zimbabwean government is not efficient in issuing passports and because the South African government is not operating an open-door policy towards migrants from Zimbabwe. It is perfectly plausible to say of such Zimbabwean migrants that they are fully supportive of the ethic embedded in the two anarchies. They support civilian rights in global civil society and citizenship rights within the society of sovereign states. They would normally support the right of a sovereign state like South Africa to control is borders. Yet, in these circumstances, it is possible to interpret their illegal migration not as undermining the values of the constitutive practices but as demonstrating their commitment to them. They are leaving because both their civilian rights and their citizenship rights are not being respected in Zimbabwe. As things currently stand in Zimbabwe these rights are merely notional, not real. Through leaving Zimbabwe, often by dangerous and circuitous routes, they are affirming the core values of the global practices. Here their illegal conduct confirms and affirms the core values of our global institutions.

Let us consider another set of circumstances which might lead us to assess illegal migrants as upholding, rather than infringing, the core values of the double anarchy. This set is to be found where such migration is brought about not by tyrannical or authoritarian states but by quasi-states, weak states or failed states.[17] People might flee such states because such states fail to provide protection for civilian rights or citizenship rights. This has happened in any number of African states that are unable to provide rights protection for their citizens. At times it has happened in Mozambique, Angola, the

17 There is an ongoing dispute among academics about how best to understand such states. I cannot go into the details of this now. For an introduction to the notion of quasi-states see Jackson, 1990.

Peoples Republic of Congo, Rwanda, Burundi, Somalia, Sudan, Chad, Zimbabwe and elsewhere. Here once again the people fleeing might tacitly or overtly spell out their support for civilian and citizenship rights, yet maintain that they have fled from places where these rights are notional and not real. The people currently fleeing to Spain from the states of north west Africa can plausibly make just such a case. Here, then, it would be wrong to simply characterize the migrants' act of illegal entry into another state as both illegal and unethical. For although their action is without doubt illegal, in the technical sense that they have not adhered to the letter of the law, their action can be interpreted as reaffirming the core values of the greater practices within which it is taking place. Through their flight they endorse the core values of global civil society and the society of sovereign states.

Yet another class of case where illegal migration might be understood as ethical needs to be mentioned. I am referring to what have come to be called 'economic migrants'. Such migrants enter a state illegally in search of work. Here the push factor might not come from tyranny or from state failure but from a lack of market opportunity in the home state. Consider the case of workers from Mexico who gain illegal entry into the territory of the USA. Such workers might claim their illegal action to be ethical. They might make the case that they are using their civilian rights (these include their right to freedom of movement, right to property in their own labour, right to freedom of association and so on) to seek out other civilians across the border with whom they can strike up mutually beneficial contracts. They do this knowing that, from the point of view of civil society, there are no borders. Mexican civilians who live in Mexico move to the USA to seek civilians there who are prepared to employ them. That mutually beneficial contracts are made demonstrates that both parties endorse and uphold the values of civil society. Such migrants can also show, through what they say and what they do, that they pose no threat to the values implicit in the society of sovereign states. While in the USA they respect the laws of the land, the rights of USA citizens and so on. They pay their taxes. They make it clear that they pose no threat whatsoever to national security or the national interest of the USA. Indeed, if expanding GDP is a national interest, they actively contribute to achieving it. They actively seek to benefit the economy and the society of the

USA. On this interpretation what wrongdoing there is must be understood to have been committed by the USA government in forging its migration policy. When states grant amnesty to illegal migrants who have been in a state for some time this must be read as an acknowledgement of the above – an acknowledgement that the migrants have been good civilians and that they will continue to be good citizens.[18]

Once the arrival of illegal immigrants is understood in the ways outlined in the examples above, where the illegal act of migrating can be construed as supportive of the ethical underpinnings of the global practices, then policy-makers and citizens considering an appropriate response to such migrants will have to think about them in ways that are distinctly different to their normal ways. The standard reaction by citizens and policy-makers to illegal immigrants is to think of them as wrongdoers (criminals of a kind) who ought to be apprehended and sent back from whence they came. Furthermore, it is often taken for granted that measures should be taken to ensure that steps are taken to prevent easy access in future. Recommended measures often include stricter border controls, better border surveillance and the construction of physical barriers to entry (walls, fences, lights and so on). On the alternative interpretations that we have been considering, a completely different set of responses is called for. On these interpretations, to treat illegal migrants simply as wrongdoers and criminals would clearly be wrong.[19] If we were to give an account of the Zimbabweans who are entering South Africa illegally that portrayed them not as people who are undermining the core practices within which they are participating but as supporting the core values which underpin them, then a policy of seeking to apprehend and repatriate such people would clearly be inappropriate. Doing this would undermine the international standing of the South African government. Some alternative arrangement has to be made for such people. Furthermore, this assessment also points to the need for the South African government and the governments of other

18 The USA Congress is currently considering a bill which would grant amnesty to millions of illegal immigrants. The assessment guiding the production of this law, it seems reasonable to assume, must be similar to the argument provided here.

19 It would be as wrong to treat them as criminals as it would be to treat someone who burst into one's house while fleeing from a would-be murderer as a housebreaker.

states in the society of states to undertake action aimed at preventing the rights abuse taking place in Zimbabwe.

The assessment of the illegal migrancy from Zimbabwe to South Africa offered above indicates a clear set of guidelines about what an appropriate response might be. It suggests that the problem is not simply one of 'How should we treat these migrants here and now?', although it certainly requires an answer to that question, but is a wider one to do with rights-abusing rule by the government of a sovereign 'democratic' state, and also to do with state failure (with the failure of the Zimbabwean state to provide even the most elementary of the services that citizens are entitled to expect). The failures of the Zimbabwean government are causing ethical harm to the people living there and forcing them to seek protection for their core values in neighbouring states. What constitutive theory does here is alert us to an ethical history which helps us make sense of illegal acts by millions of people who, it is fair to assume, would normally never dream of acting contrary to the ethically-sanctioned laws of the global practices.[20]

This assessment points to the requirement that South Africa and other states in the society of states consider their own role with regard to the Zimbabwean state. The questions to be considered are complex ones to do with the reasons for the failure of the Zimbabwean state which has brought about the exodus of people from that state. The theory suggests that other states in the society of states should consider to what extent their actions or inactions have brought about the failure of the Zimbabwean state. There are two significant lines of questioning that could be pursued here: First, has the society of states through its actions undermined the ability of the Zimbabwean state to do what is ethically required of it? Clearly, if the answer to this were positive, then in a real sense the exodus could (at one remove) be blamed on what the international community had or had not done to support the Zimbabwean government. President Mugabe has repeatedly claimed just this, arguing that Britain, in particular, reneged on its promise to provide funding for the orderly transfer of land from a minority white elite to black Zimbabweans. When this was not forthcoming he had to resort to

---

20 As things currently stand (February 2008) almost a quarter of the total population of Zimbabwe has migrated to South Africa.

other measures to deal with the pressure for land from citizens. In particular, he resorted to force. This in turn brought down international sanctions on his government and made the economy weaker. At present it is one of the weakest economies in the world. On this argument state failure was brought about by the initial set of broken promises by the international community. Part of the cause of the flood of refugees to South Africa can, on this argument, be laid at the door of the international community.

Is this a good argument? I believe not. A close look at the interactions of the Mugabe government with the international community over the past two decades shows that there have been repeated grants of aid to facilitate land redistribution within Zimbabwe. But the aid was not put to use for this purpose, but instead was used by President Mugabe's regime to buy political support. The flow of aid was slowed and then halted only as a result of the corruption and mismanagement of the Zimbabwean government. The ethical history undermines the ethical allegations made by the Mugabe regime.

There is a second and quite different line of questioning that can be pursued here. The international liberal press is currently pursuing this tack with great vigour. According to this view, the international community (in particular, South Africa) is guilty of an ethical failure in not having brought sufficient pressure to bear on President Mugabe to modify his autocratic behaviour. On this argument the South African government possesses sufficient leverage on the Zimbabwean government which, once activated, could easily force Mugabe to cease most of his autocratic policies. In support of this many have pointed out that in 1979, when the South African government finally decided that the time had come for the minority white regime of Prime Minister Ian Smith to negotiate a hand-over of political power to the black majority, it applied the necessary pressure and within weeks Mr Smith went to Lancaster House to negotiate with Robert Mugabe and Joshua Nkomo about an end to white rule. On this view it would be easy for the South African government to bring about a similar result if it were only prepared to display sufficient political will. The leverage to be used is to be found in South Africa's control of the major transport links with Zimbabwe. Curtailing these would limit the supply of energy (oil and coal) and threaten most of the country's exports. This, it is alleged, would soon change the behaviour of the government.

What are we to make of this assessment? In terms of the background theory set out here, we ought to evaluate it as follows. The test of the assessment is twofold: Does it take seriously the values embedded in the society of states, in particular sovereignty and the value of pluralism? Second, does it take seriously the civilian rights of the people in Zimbabwe? The most prominent component of those providing this assessment is that which draws attention to the human rights abuses taking place in Zimbabwe. So the assessment cannot be faulted on this ground. The assessment also shows respect for the sovereignty of the state. In no way can the assessment be construed as advocating the denial of sovereignty to Zimbabwe in the long run. Also, what is recommended is not a policy which is aimed at enriching the South African state. Indeed, in the short run the sanctions proposed will impose a severe cost on the South African state. This assessment then, overall, is a strong one. A strong neighbouring state which failed to act in these circumstances could be construed as committing an ethical wrong – the wrong of not taking the civilian rights of Zimbabweans seriously and also not taking the citizenship rights of Zimbabweans seriously. The latter are being systematically abused by President Mugabe through repeated crackdowns on all forms of legitimate political dissent.

I shall not go any further into the details of the Zimbabwean case. This would involve writing another monograph. For the moment I wish to highlight once again how this kind of ethics-centred international analysis produces readings of a given situation that are ethically rich at every point. The assessments of a given state of affairs using this approach require us to explore competing ethical histories of action and interaction that have led up to the present 'state of play'. These in turn steer us towards certain policy prescriptions. In the present instance the first reading of the causes of state failure in Zimbabwe (broken promises by the community of states) suggests a forward-looking policy which would prescribe honouring the earlier financial commitments and indeed increasing them. The alternative reading (Zimbabwe is still an autocratic rights-abusing state because the international community, especially South Africa, have failed to apply sufficiently stiff sanctions to the Zimbabwean government) suggests a contrary line of policy – it suggests increasing sanctions against Zimbabwe to force a change of behaviour. In each case the initial reading of the situation is ethically loaded and the ethical dimension is present all the way through to the policy prescription phase.

What we have seen in this discussion of the phenomenon of illegal migrancy is the way in which constitutive theory allows an assessment that takes seriously our participation in the double anarchy. By applying the method to illegal migrants entering South Africa from Zimbabwe we have seen how we have to assess our relationship to them taking into account the ethical salience of the fact that we are all both civilians and citizens in the dynamic double anarchy. It showed how acts that, on the surface appear to be straight instances of wrongdoing, need to be interpreted in the light of the ethical history of the migrants concerned. Importantly, it shows how an exploration of this history might implicate us in ways that require of us that we make some complex and fine ethical judgements. If the migrants' illegal actions are a result of our own failure to do something (a failure to keep our promises or a failure to impose appropriate sanctions), then this locates their action in a specific ethical framework that requires of us a specific ethically informed response.

Crucially, what constitutive theory has shown in this example is how in analysing our relationship to the migrants we ought to pay attention to two discrete but interlinked ethical features of the relationship. First, we ought to consider our relationship to them in terms of the rules and norms of civil society – that borderless global society within which we constitute one another as rights holders. What is our ethical history here? What does this history point to as an appropriate response? Second, it requires that we have to consider our relationship to the migrants in their capacity as fellow citizens in the society of sovereign states. As citizens of Zimbabwe are they to be understood as wrongdoers in crossing illegally into the territory of South African citizens? Or are there circumstances in which the citizens of a foreign state might be justified in doing this?[21] In short,

---

21 As we saw earlier there are some circumstances when breaking a well-known rule might be a way of demonstrating one's commitment to the core values of the practice within which the rule is located. This happens, for example, when states withhold payment of the dues to an international organization with a view to getting the organization to uphold its core values. We might call this manoeuvre *mobilizing negativity*.

the theory enables us to get to grips with the ethical complexities presented to us as participants in two related global anarchies.

ASSESSING HUMANITARIAN INTERVENTION

Let us consider another aspect of contemporary international relations that can be better understood by using constitutive theory – an ethics-centred approach to international affairs.[22]

During the Cold War international politics was often understood to be built around a bipolar balance of power backed by a finely balanced system of nuclear deterrence between the two superpowers. Under that system any project involving military interference in the domestic affairs of another state had to be weighed with a careful view as to how it might influence the nuclear balance. Once the bipolar world had ended, it seemed safe for militarily strong states to consider military intervention in the affairs of other states in order to stop or prevent gross human rights violations. This was something that certain states had the capacity to do. Given that this was now possible, the question arose: When would such intervention be justified? Also, where interventions took place, how were they to be interpreted? Underlying these questions was a major concern which might be stated as follows: Did the emergence of a practice of humanitarian intervention signal the coming into being of a new international order in which the sovereignty norm which had been at the heart of the international system since the Treaty of Westphalia was eroded? Or, to put it differently, do states which launch acts of humanitarian intervention that involve military action within the territory of a foreign sovereign state threaten the sovereignty norm which is at the core of the international society of sovereign states? On the face of the matter it would seem that acts of humanitarian intervention are contrary to the non-intervention rule. States which mount interventions must be seen as reneging on their commitment to the sovereignty principle.

Here again, though, those assessments which suggest that in the modern world we stand before a radical choice, to uphold the sovereignty norm or to protect human rights, are wide of the mark. Constitutive theory offers us an alternative reading of intervention,

22 On humanitarian intervention generally see Holzgrefe and Keohane 2003.

one that takes seriously that we are simultaneously participants in two global practices. It recommends understanding such actions within the context of the two anarchies that are central to contemporary world politics. The point could be made with reference to any of the interventions that have taken place recently, such as those in Haiti, Somalia, Sierra Leone, Bosnia-Herzegovina, Kosovo, East Timor, Afghanistan and Iraq.

In order to give a proper account of these interventions what has to be considered are the ethical histories of each case taking into account that the actors involved are participants in both global civil society and the society of sovereign states. The actions of the interveners and those being intervened upon have to be interpreted within the context of the double anarchy. In seeking a good interpretation the relevant questions to ask are: Prior to the intervention was the target state in good ethical standing from the point of view of both anarchical societies? There are two sub-questions that follow from this: Was the target state (and the people within it) protecting the civilian rights of the people in its territory and those further afield? Was the target state protective of the rights of its own citizens and the citizens of other states? Imagine having to interpret an intervention where the answer to all these questions was a positive one. If it could be established that the target state actively protected the civilian rights of people in its territory and protected their citizenship rights (this includes the citizenship rights of its own citizens and the citizenship rights of people from other sovereign states), then, of any military intervention that took place, we would have to assess it as an act of aggression against both the values of global civil society and the values protected by the society of sovereign states. Presumably, we would reach this conclusion were the Netherlands to intervene militarily in the domestic affairs of present-day Belgium. This would not be humanitarian intervention but straightforward aggression. This judgement would apply no matter what the intervener said in justification of the act of intervention.[23]

Consider as an example, the NATO intervention into Bosnia in 1994. If one were requested to give an account of that action, there

---

23 An actor's own description of his/her/its act is not definitive of the action in question. The actor might lie, might attempt a spurious rationalization or, indeed, might misunderstand his own action.

are a number of possible interpretations that could be offered. The one offered by the Serbian government under Slobodan Milosevic was that NATO was guilty of armed aggression against a sovereign state. He claimed that the dispute with the Bosnians was an internal matter and the international community had no right to intervene. Another possible interpretation was that the internal war in Serbia was a threat to international peace and security between states and that this warranted military intervention as authorized by Chapter 7 of the UN Charter. A third possibility was to interpret what was done there as an act of humanitarian intervention that upheld the standards internal to both global civil society and the society of sovereign states.

What are we to make of these three possible accounts? According to constitutive theory the first interpretation fails for it does not take seriously the obligation on states to protect the civilian rights of people in their territories. The second also fails for it makes reference only to inter-state relationships and says nothing about the abuse of human rights in the conflict – it says nothing about the abuse of civilian rights in the context of global civil society. The first two interpretations are unsatisfactory because they leave out of account ethically significant features of the circumstances that pertained in that place at that time. Here once again we see that the strength of constitutive theory lies in the way it uncovers ethical *omissions* in rival theories. It is important to remember that those offering the erroneous interpretations are not merely guilty of making a faulty social analysis but, by offering such interpretations, are doing something ethically wrong. According to the ethics-centred approach to international relations being presented here, making erroneous analyses is in itself ethical wrongdoing. It is to present a theory which, if accepted and acted upon, would undermine the ethics embedded in the global constitution within which the actors (including the social analysts) are constructed as who they value themselves to be.[24]

24 The analysts of international affairs are themselves participants in the global practices that they (and we) are examining. If their analyses can be shown to undermine the core values of the practices in which they are participating, then they are guilty of an ethical failure. Their act of producing such a theory erodes the ethical standing they enjoy in these global practices. For example, analyses such as realist ones, which fail to pay due attention to the global practice within which we are constituted as individual holders of civilian rights, undermine this latter

ASSESSING GLOBALIZATION

Let us see how the ethics-centred form of analysis being used here might throw light on that major phenomenon of our time that we often refer to as 'globalization'. Key features of this phenomenon, which we all experience in one way or another, are widely agreed to involve a speeding-up of time that leads to a shrinking of space, which, in turn, results in the de-territorialization of a whole host of activities. Consider the manufacturing of commodities. Where once the whole process was concentrated in specific geographic localities, now because of the speed and ease of communications, it is often spread out and divided up around the world. Where once the factors of production (capital, labour and material) were all sourced locally, they now often come from a wide variety of places. Where production and markets were once closely tied to a specific region, this is often no longer the case. In the modern world many aspects of culture and fashion are no longer local, but are internationally mobile. Fashions in music, clothing, cinema, television are dispersed globally. The well-known phrase 'the McDonaldization of the world' captures something of what is happening here. Where once almost all a person's social networks were local, many are now transnational. Similarly, with regard to education, where once primary, secondary and tertiary education might take place locally, for many people this is no longer true.

It is now widely recognized that globalization is bringing about (even forcing) change to many traditional social institutions. These include families, tribes, clans, churches, educational institutions, companies, states and international organizations. On the face of the matter globalization appears to be an irresistible force which is bringing about changes to (some would even stay 'threatens to destroy') any number of traditional forms of human association.[25]

Although there is agreement that something like globalization is happening, there is much contention amongst scholars about how best to explain and understand it. Some explain it with reference to the spread and intensification of a liberal global economic order.

---

practice. For a rights holder to do this is to do something ethically wrong. It is wrong in that it leads the author of the analysis, and those who act on the analysis, to adopt policies that do not take the rights of civilians seriously.

25 On the destructive potential of globalized capital see Polanyi, 1957.

According to the liberal account of this process, the spread of a global free market, within which individuals and associations of individuals (corporations) are left free to pursue their own interests, will promote both democracy and peace between democratic states.[26] An alternative account also notes the spread of the liberal global economic order, but interprets this as being destructive of the states system as we know it. Thinkers promoting it see the process of globalization as being one that makes the maintenance of state sovereignty problematic. The spread of capitalist relations has made sovereign state borders ever less salient than they have been in the past. As this is happening what emerges are different kinds of social authorities which, taken together, produce what might be called a post-Westphalian order. The emerging overlapping tapestry of authorities form what some have termed a new feudalism.[27]

Yet another interpretation of the globalizing process is to be found in the writings of Karl Marx and those who have continued his tradition. Roughly speaking the line pursued by such writers is that the global capitalist system is so powerful that it drives out traditional forms of authority and is the driving force behind the conduct of modern sovereign states. Far from generating a global harmony of interests, the spread of this social arrangement guarantees ongoing international conflict between states and in the long run will bring about the downfall of the international system as we know it.[28] A related but different take on the subject is to be found in the work of a modern Hegelian, Francis Fukuyama, who argues that the process of globalization has brought us to the end of history. On his view we now have a global capitalist economic order firmly in place and also a system of democratic sovereign states. The economic order and the political one together form a stable international order which faces no fundamental challenges at all (Fukuyama, 1992). We have reached, he claims, the end of history. Others portray it has having to do with not only the spread of capitalism but also with the

---

26 Influential thinkers who launched the tradition include Adam Smith, John Stuart Mill, Jeremy Bentham and Richard Cobden. The most influential liberal statesman was Woodrow Wilson. For a clear statement of the strands of liberal thinking today see Bayliss & Smith, 2006, Chapter 8.

27 A key modern writer pursuing this line of thought is Andrew Linklater. See Linklater, 1998.

28 An influential writer in this tradition was of course Lenin (Lenin, 1977).

spread of a set of Western cultural ideas, especially those to do with human rights. However, no matter what different explanations are offered, there seems to be a rough consensus about what might be called 'the fact of globalization' (Held & McClure, 2000; Shaw, 1994). Globalization is happening and there is wide agreement that the fact of globalization has presented us with an imperative to rethink some of our entrenched normative political ideas. In particular, it is suggested that we need to rethink our ideas about sovereignty and democracy. It seems that the forces of globalization are posing a threat to the sovereign authority of states as we know them (Shaw, 1999, p. 2). *A fortiori*, globalization also threatens the democracy that exists within many of our states. Where once the democratically elected governments could control and regulate market forces in ways that benefited the citizens in those states, it now seems as if transnational forces not under the control of democratic governments can threaten citizens' interests.

How we answer the normative questions presented to us by globalization depends on how we understand the ethical dimensions of the process. What is called for is an ethically informed account of this phenomenon. Providing such an account is particularly difficult for what we are called upon to interpret here is not the action (or series of actions) of a specified actor, be it an individual, a state or an international organization, but the interactions of all the participants in global civil society. When considering the ethical dimensions of globalization what we are focused on is a process that consists of the interactions of several billion people worldwide who are participants in the process. Taken together the participants do not form a collective actor pursuing some common goal. Quite the contrary, the participants are pursuing their self-interests.

The rival accounts briefly outlined above all present us with a set of ethical judgements about how we ought to understand globalization and about what we ought to do in the face of it. The liberal assessment portrays the spread of a capitalist economic order as an ethical advance which promotes the expansion of a human rights-based social formation and displaces more primitive and less individualistic social forms. On this view the spread of a liberal economic order will lead in time to modernization and the establishment of democratic states. For those who are convinced of such accounts of globalization, the process must, of course, be judged to be an ethically good one. It follows, also, that promoting globalization is the right thing to do from an ethical point of view.

In sharp contrast to this are Marxian materialist analyses which present the spread of capitalist social relations worldwide as destructive of public authorities of all kind, including democratic ones. According to this line of thinking, the empire of global civil society results in the privatization of control over a whole lot of goods which ought to be under public authority. On this view, globalization is an ethically noxious process which, for ethical reasons, we ought to oppose at every point. Such analyses call on us to embark on political action to halt it. According to this view, the anti-globalization 'Battle in Seattle' was ethically admirable.

Yet another account is that produced by realists who argue that globalization is a process that only proceeds insofar as states in the system of sovereign states allow it to happen. The ethical implication is that there may well be occasions when states would be ethically justified in curtailing and regulating the global market.

What are we to make of these contrasting accounts of globalization? Is globalization a force for the good as suggested by liberal analyses? – is it a force that advances human rights and democracy? Or, does globalization leave the system of states essentially untouched as argued by realists? Or, is globalization a force which is systematically destroying the public places for democratic politics as argued by structural analyses of a Marxian kind? As a preliminary step, before we attempt to answer these questions, we need to point out two common features of the accounts presented above. First, they all present globalization as a process with powerful structural effects. These are not the result of millions of people acting together in pursuit of a common purpose. Rather the effects derive from the structure of interaction between individuals in global civil society. The participants in GCS do not form a collective actor but are private individuals pursuing their own self-interest. Second, the accounts all make ethical judgements about the outcome of the forces of globalization – it advances human rights or it undermines sovereignty and politics, and so on.

At this point it appears, once again, that we are confronted with the choice that we discussed earlier when considering both illegal migration and humanitarian intervention. On the one hand are those who are in favour of the expansion of global civil society. This group falls into the school advocating a cosmopolitan approach to global ethics. These theorists say that the interconnectedness of international life is now such that we have to move on from our traditional preoccupation with the modes of governance within our traditional territorial units. We now ought to pay more attention to developing theories of transnational justice and to developing a democratic theory that is not confined to democracy within nation states. The bedrock of such theories should now be notions of individual human rights.

On the other hand there are the communitarians who, while acknowledging that important changes have taken place in the international domain, still insist that our ethical commitments are, and should be, focused on our immediate political communities (in most cases these would be our national communities encompassed within states). For such people the protection of the sovereignty of such communities is still a major ethical concern. The values people hold dear are those constituted within such communities; therefore it is important to defend their independence.

It appears then that 'the fact of globalization', the fact of the structural power of global civil society, has presented us with a radical choice between cosmopolitanism and communitarianism. The cosmopolitan view is one that directs us to advocate an expansion of capitalism through the opening-up of world markets. State boundaries ought to become less important. Protectionist policies should be eschewed. There should be free flows of capital, goods and labour. On this view, individuals know best where their interests lie and they ought to be free to pursue them, no matter where this pursuit takes them. On the communitarian view it is right and proper that political communities (normally understood as states or nations) ought to be allowed to protect themselves against the forces that have been unleashed by global capitalism.

The standard but conflicting approaches sketched above present globalization as an empirical given, as something that is happening to us as an unintended consequence of what we have done in the past. It is a consequence of industrialization, modernization and the spread of a capitalist economic order. We are to understand it as a worldwide process to which we humans are being subjected. Its consequences are unintended, but structurally determined by the rules of interaction in global civil society. The accounts given differ in the ethical evaluation they make of the outcomes of globalization. It appears, then, when we are confronted with these rival accounts, we have to choose between a cosmopolitan approach or a communitarian one – we have to choose between individual rights and states rights. Do we have to make this radical ethical choice or is there an alternative account of globalization which does not require this?

The approaches we have considered so far present globalization as an empirical process the outcome of which we can now consider controlling in terms of one or another ethical code that we might choose. The analysis of the process itself, though, in all these accounts is not an ethics-centred one. It is not one that places the investigator and those being investigated as participants in a common ethically-based practice.

In contrast to this line of thought, constitutive theory suggests that the features commonly brought together under the umbrella term 'globalization', such as speed, interconnectedness, shrinking space, global division of labour, instant communication and so on, are what is produced by an existing global practice with its associated embedded ethic. These are not the consequences of the operation of social processes not yet under ethical, political and legal control, but are the manifestations of an already operational ethically-based practice. The outcomes referred to are the result of the emergence, intensification and continued operation of a highly successful global civil society within which we are constituted as participating rights holders. Where the common understandings of globalization would see it as a social force that still has to be brought into one or another ethically-based framework (cosmopolitan or communitarian), constitutive theory sees it as evidence of an ethically-based framework already in operation.

To repeat, according to constitutive theory, globalization is not something that has come upon us (in the way that pollution has) and which now presents us with the problem of finding a suitable normative framework to regulate it – that would include a set of ethical commitments, political arrangements, legal systems and social institutions. Rather, the features referred to must be understood as providing us with evidence of an already existing global social practice within which important ethical values are brought into being. This follows from the core insight on which constitutive theory is based, which is that the analysis of social phenomena must always start with an examination of what has been ethically achieved by the people under investigation. It starts with the assumption that all social relations are ethical achievements.[29]

Once globalization is understood as the functioning of an already realized ethically-based social whole, then the problems it poses for us, who are participants in it, appear in a different light. No longer should we think of globalization as some external process that has emerged amongst us and which is in a period of more or less uncontrolled growth, and that needs to be tamed and restrained. It is not some external force to which we have to devise an ethical response. Rather it emerges as a set of consequences that have arisen from a global social practice within which we are constituted as ethically valued beings – rights holders. In a nutshell, the facts of globalization are produced by the dynamics of our ethical conduct.

On the view being presented here, if we wish to understand globalization, we must not start off with a consideration of its effects (shrinking of space, velocity of interactions and multiple interconnections) but with a consideration of the actors, their actions and the practice within which they take place together with an examination of the ethic embedded in that practice. Globalization refers to the total set of actions and interactions by individual rights holders in global civil society. Some are owners of only their labour and their involvement in the globalized world is as sellers of that labour; others are owners of capital and their involvement is through the investment of that asset. Some use their rights to pursue educational projects, while others pursue religious connections with other rights holders; some travel the world as tourists, while others are internationally mobile as entertainers or as sportsmen and -women. A defining characteristic of the actors in this global civil society is that their basic identity in this practice is that of a private rights holder – a civilian. In this sphere of activity the interactions and contracts

---

29 This is a definitional link. The truth of this assertion is part of what we mean when we refer to 'social relations'. If a set of relationships between people is not ethically based then the relationships between them are not social ones but are relationships between objects. Social relationships exist between people when they assess, evaluate, account for, understand, explain, justify and rationalize their conduct (and the conduct of others) to one another in terms of ethically-based rules which specify what is to count as 'doing good', 'committing a wrong', 'behaving properly' and 'being guilty of misconduct'.

take place without drawing upon authority granted to the actor by territorially defined sovereign states. From the point of view of any given civilian the status of any fellow civilian is not determined by his or her membership of a family, church, nation, clan, tribe, ethnic group or race. *Qua* civilian it does not matter whether the co-participant is Eskimo, Black, Islamic, Jewish or Belgian. What matters is that the civilian is a rights holder in good standing in the borderless global civil society.

The interactions of civilians on a global scale have brought about (and will continue to bring about) the changes that are always listed in the mainstream literature and websites dealing with globalization. Civilians are increasingly making meaningful and profitable connections without giving any particular ethical significance to cultural, political, religious, economic and social borders. The borders that are being disregarded by civilians were traditionally of major importance in international and inter-societal relations. The interactions of civilians, when seen in a global context, have brought about new constellations of power and influence. They have brought about new distributions of privilege and poverty. They have brought about dialogues across religions and cultures. They have brought into being many new hybrid forms of society. One prominent manifestation of this is the multiple diasporic communities that have sprung up around the world.

If globalization is the product of a functioning ethically-based global practice within which we are all participants, why is it often perceived to be such a problem? Why is so much attention being paid to this phenomenon? Constitutive theory indicates that it is a problem, not because it is some new social force not yet tamed by ethically sound social institutions but because we who are constituted as ethical actors (as civilians) in it, are at the same time constituted as citizens in a different global institution, the society of sovereign states. It is our simultaneous participation in both rapidly changing practices that has produced the ethical problems we are experiencing. Given that we are constituted as who we value ourselves to be in both practices, we are not faced with a choice between them (in the way that one might be faced with the choice of which club to join), but instead have to understand that, in the face of social change, there has emerged a tension between our roles as civilians and our roles as citizens. The tension indicates the need for internal adjustments and a general harmonization between the two practices. If, as we have seen above, civil society and the society of sovereign states are intimately related to one another such that the one is foundational for the other, then the tensions we have been discussing must indicate emerging incoherencies with these practices. The problem posed for us by globalization is essentially an ethical one to do with what, on the face of it, appears to be a fundamental tension within the social practices in which we are constituted as free individuals.

To put the matter another way, on the analysis being given here, globalization is to be understood as the intensification and extension of the ethical practice within which most people worldwide are constituted as rights holders (or, as we have called them here, civilians). Globalization has emerged as a problem because it often appears to conflict with what people are entitled to do as citizens within the society of sovereign states. The problem presented to us is, at base, a problem of co-ordinating ethical practices that have fallen out of harmony with one another.

This is not the first time that we have confronted this particular ethical difficulty. What has re-emerged in the globalized world is the same set of problems that originally beset local civil societies and which were overcome through the creation of states (and in particular democratic states). Earlier I mentioned that while the emergence of civil society could be seen as positive from an ethical point of view, in that it created a society of rights holders, it had an ethical 'downside' in that it produced participants who were caught in an never-ending set of competitive, alienated and unequal power relations. I mentioned how these defects of civil society were remedied through the creation of states within which people, who as civilians were competitive, alienated and unequal, came to constitute one another in the new role of citizen in a sovereign (and at best democratic) state. In this new role people recognized one another as persons of equal worth, they had a common concern with the pursuit of the national interest and they could make use of their national government to bring about a reduction in the inequality. Furthermore, their respective sovereign states were recognized as autonomous within the society of states.

Globalization has reproduced the set of problems we initially experienced in our local civil societies, but now the problem has been produced on a global scale. Civilians in the borderless global civil society are now experiencing ever more extreme forms of the short-comings mentioned. The competition in the global market is ever more cut-throat. The price of labour is being driven down by the plentiful supply of labour – in particular by the people of China who have only recently joined global civil society. No matter where one is located in GCS one is exposed to competition from all the other rights holders in it, no matter where they happen to be. Thus, wage labour in the USA and the EU, for example, is feeling itself to be vulnerable to the competition emanating from many states in Asia. For the people in Africa the situation is, if anything, worse. The communication systems, educational arrangements and basic infra-structures are so poor that the civilians who would like more success in the world market find it difficult to achieve. In GCS the alienation between people who live close to one another is bad, but it is even worse for those civilians who are on opposite sides of the world.[30]

Finally, the operation of global civil society is producing inequal-ities on a massive scale in many different areas of activity within GCS. Wealth, income, ownership, jobs, educational opportunities, opportunities for leisure time activities and so on are all very unequally distributed. Crucially, the overall pattern of outcomes which strikes us as ethically noxious are not the result of ethical wrongdoing on the part of any particular person or group of people. They are the result of civilians making good and proper use of their civilian rights. Of course, here and there, rights abusers are to be found; these are people who have gained personal advantage through their wrongdoing, but the overall pattern being discussed here is not the result of their actions but is the outcome of the structural con-straints internal to GCS.

In our earlier discussion we saw how the ethical problems encountered in local, geographically specific, civil societies were solved through the emergence of sovereign states in the society of

---

30 There are many different facets to the alienation that rights holders' experience in civil society. These include alienation of workers from the product of their labour, alienation from the owners of the plant that they use in the production of what they produce, alienation from their fellow workers, alienation from those who finally come to purchase whatever it is that has been produced, alienation from the end users of such products. I cannot go into a fully-fledged discussion of these interesting distinctions here.

such states. In states alienated civilians were united as citizens; in states competition gave way to forms of co-operation and in states key inequalities could be tackled through the redistributive policies of governments. Now that civil society has expanded to encompass the world, the question is whether such problems can be overcome globally? There appear to be insuperable problems here. On the initial account of how the problems of civil society were solved, which was presented above, a key feature of the solution was that civilians who were constituted as independent competitive actors in civil society were brought together as citizens in a sovereign state with a single government. Within the sovereign state redistributions could be brought about by the government. The ethical advances alluded to seemed plausible when considering the case of a single state. However, the ethical advances alluded to seem implausible when considering, not a single state, but a whole society of sovereign states. For in such an arrangement (the one that we in fact have) the states are in competition with one another for scarce resources, for skilled people, for access to specific markets, for control of the processes of production of particular commodities and so on. On the face of it, it would seem that a system of sovereign states would aggravate the competition between people found in global civil society and the alienation produced in it. Instead of creating fraternity to replace alienation, the society of sovereign states would seem well suited to simply sharpening the ethical shortcomings of GCS that we have identified.[31]

It might be thought that a possible solution to the ethical problems experienced in GCS might be through the creation of a single global state. But there are several problems to be considered here. First, at present there is no such state and it seems unlikely that one will emerge soon. Second, even if a world state were to emerge, it could not achieve one of the key goods achieved within the society of sovereign states, which, as we saw earlier in the book, is the institutional framework within which free political communities are constituted as free states. A world state would put in place a single concentrated form of power and authority. It would be difficult to portray this as an ethical advancement that secured freedom and diversity for political communities.

---

31 For an argument that claims that precisely this is in fact happening see Stopford & Strange, 1991.

Let me restate the ethical problem from a slightly different perspective. Whereas we can see how within single states (especially democratic ones) some of the ethical shortcomings experienced by civilians in their relationship to one another in civil society can be overcome, the solution only applies within a local part of global civil society, namely, that portion covered by that particular state. The relationships which hold between the civilians in that state and civilians elsewhere in the world remain as they were, competitive, alienated and unequal. Even if the civilians elsewhere set up their own sovereign states within which they could solve the ethical problems that existed between them, beyond the borders of their immediate states the problems would remain the same. In the system of sovereign states a fraternity is not produced, alienation and inequality across the borders of the states are not relieved and power is not equalized. The problem then is clear: How might the ethical shortcomings of global civil society (shortcomings that have been made more intense by the processes of globalization) be overcome when it (GCS) is supplemented by a system of sovereign states existing under conditions of anarchy, each pursuing its own interest?

It is at this point that a turn to the supporting philosophy of the double anarchy can help us understand the problem better and can help us get a grip on what might be done about it. The supporting philosophy indicates how the double anarchy structure provides for our constitution as free actors in two different frameworks. We are constituted as rights holders in civil society and citizens in the society of sovereign states. Also as such we are able to promote two kinds of diversity. As individual civilians we can pursue a whole range of different kinds of lives guided by quite different ideas of the good. As individual citizens we can pursue, together with the other citizens in the system of states, different ideas of what is good for our specific political communities within the system of sovereign states. In seeking a way forward to overcome the problems mentioned above, we need to find a way of preserving these values of civilianship and citizenship while solving the ethical problems identified.

I would argue that our analysis of the ethical underpinnings of the double anarchy within which we live gives a clear indication of where the solution might lie. In order to overcome the competition, alienation and inequality found in GCS, without undermining the freedom and diversity enjoyed by states in the system of sovereign states, what is called for is concerted action by the sovereign states with a view to creating another level of co-operation between them, such that the shortcomings of GCS are solved without loss of the key feature of the system of sovereign states which is that it is anarchic. How might this be done? What would such an arrangement look like?

A rough and ready example of how this might be done is provided for us by the EU. The EU has realized the ethical harmonization of two anarchical practices that we have been seeking. It is an institutional arrangement which has moved towards solving many of the problems in GCS mentioned above, while still allowing states to maintain their identities as sovereign actors entitled to pursue diverse concepts of their national good. The tension between GCS and the society of states is overcome by requiring all the member states to endorse the human rights commitments enshrined in the core documents of the union. Crucially, within the EU the member states have bound themselves not to advance 'beggar thy neighbour' policies playing off their portion of civil society against other portions located in the territories of the other member states. Also, within the EU a new level of citizenship has been established which aims to overcome the alienation civilians might feel in the European portion of GCS and to achieve a union-wide fraternity of citizens. The institutions of the EU have been able to make considerable progress in alleviating the gross inequalities that exist in the portion of GCS that falls within jurisdiction – this has been achieved in ways that cross state boundaries. So most of the ethical advance achieved by states in their domestic portions of GCS have now been achieved across state borders, but without creating a supra-state and without abolishing the sovereignty of the member states. The EU has solved key ethical problems brought about by globalizing forces in its area, but it has done so without doing away with the double anarchy which is the core practice of contemporary international relations.[32]

The way in which the EU came into being is a good example of how constitutional transformation must take place within anarchical

---

32 It is sometimes said that with the advent of the EU we are entering into what is sometimes referred to as 'a post-Westphalian' order. There is nothing wrong with this assertion provided that it is understood that it is not pointing to a new order within which the society of sovereign states is being replaced by something else. If the EU is a post-Westphalian arrangement, it must be understood that it is built on, maintains and strengthens the fundamental anarchies, GCS and the SOSS.

practices. Whatever transformations are called for have to be envisaged and brought about by the actors as constituted within the anarchical practices. In this case the relevant actors are (were) civilians and the sovereign states themselves. The process of transformation in anarchical societies must of necessity be complicated (given that the transforming outcome has to be achieved through complex multilateral actions between the participants). These will inevitably involve long and drawn-out negotiations and many compromises. The changes are likely to take longer in some parts of the anarchical societies than in others. The whole process is likely to be untidy.[33] Agreements on new structures, once reached, have to be implemented in such a way that the partners incrementally begin to trust one another. The slow and complicated processes I have outlined have indeed been the norm in the development of the EU through all its many (and ongoing) phases.

It is testimony to the success of the EU constitutional form as an ethical arrangement that there has been a consistent pressure from the states on its borders to become members of the union. In other words, civilians and citizens elsewhere see its model as a way to move beyond the tensions discussed above. Further testimony to its success is that within the EU the tensions between the role of civilian and that of citizen appear to have been solved without doing away with either of the practices within which these statuses are created. There is an open civil society within the union within which civilians can enjoy the full set of first-generation rights. They are free to move and settle where they wish.[34] This kind of movement is not seen as a threat to the sovereignty of the member states. Within the EU there have been distributions of revenues that have done much to alleviate the inequalities that existed in that part of civil society before the advent of the union. Finally the alienation experienced by these people is partially overcome through the creation of an EU citizenship. This is only partial for this citizenship still suffers from what is referred to as the 'democratic deficit'.

---

33 The contrast would be with what happens with the transformation of hierarchical practices such as states. Here there is a planning phase (constitutional convention) and a clear start date (an inauguration).

34 Although there are some constraints on the free movement of citizens for the latest tranche of new member states.

The institutional model offered to us by the EU is one that accords with the supporting philosophy of the double anarchy. The *sittlichkeit* put in place by the EU completes the ethical architecture of freedom set in place by the double anarchy. As the tensions alluded to above become increasingly pressing in the world beyond the EU it would seem to me that, insofar as people as civilians and citizens wish to resolve those tensions, they will have to come together to consider embarking on political processes that take them towards EU-type solutions.

What I have suggested above is not a utopian idea divorced from reality. Given the ethical structure of contemporary international practices, a failure to move in the direction indicated will plunge those who fail to make the necessary political initiatives into positions of increasing weakness caused by a loss of ethical standing by all the participants within the existing anarchical international practices. This will, in turn, have long-term effects on their political power. As globalization forges ahead, the ethical shortcomings of civil society will become ever more manifest. Here is a brief list of how this might happen: First, the competition between workers in global civil society located in different parts of the world will become ever more acrimonious. Those in well-paid jobs in all sectors of the global economy will feel the competition from the newly active civilians in Asia and elsewhere increasingly keenly. They will be tempted to call on their governments to pass legislation to protect 'their' jobs. Insofar as governments do this, they and those who support them will be shown to have but a shallow commitment to the values embedded in civil society. Their actions will show a lack of respect for the rights of civilians in other parts of global civil society. Their moral standing in global civil society will fall. This initial loss of standing will become worse if the governments of these states (and their supporters) start using force to protect their jobs ('their rights') and resources. Also, those whose rights are not taken seriously during this process, are likely to mobilize in many different ways against the actions of those seen to be unjust in terms of the standard human rights discourse that underpins GCS. When the protectionist states that deny others their civilian rights move beyond their territories in search of the raw materials necessary for what they produce, insofar as they do not generally respect other people's civil rights they will be regarded as plunderers, occupiers and imperialists. This will further undermine their ethical standing in the international practices and will once again provide others with a nodal point around which to mobilize political action against such actors. The political campaigns that materialize might use tools that range from non-violent sanctions to the methods of global terror. These methods of protest are not powerful in themselves, but, when they build on a strong ethical case, they will draw in increasing political support.

Second, the alienation between civilians in different parts of GCS will become progressively more acute. The sense of unfairness between the 'haves' and the 'have-nots' will increase. If this goes too far, it will reduce participants' commitment to the constitutive, human rights norms of GCS. In its place people might turn to other divisive ways of being in the world, ways which do not involve any kind of global society, but instead involve people simply committing to local social arrangements based on religion, aesthetic consider-ations, tribal loyalties, warlordism and so on. The relations between such actors might end up not being social relations at all, but might turn out to be a set of crude encounters based on nothing but force.

The developments outlined might also lead to civilians in deprived areas seeking to use the power of their states to advance their particularist interests. This could well result in imperial wars between states which in turn would start destroying the ethicality embedded in the society of states.

The important feature of this analysis of globalization to keep in mind is that it seeks to advance our understanding of both short- and long-term international processes by focusing on the ethical dimen-sions of our common international life. What this analysis shows is that globalization cannot properly be understood as a problem that can be confronted by any single civilian, citizen or state. Globalization is presenting us with macro ethical problems to do with tensions internal to the existing global practices. Any solution to these will have to involve international actors acting in concert to erect supplementary institutional structures to deal with them. An assess-ment of globalization based on constitutive theory requires that the states involved in the system of sovereign states take seriously the plight of those parts of global civil society that are not flourishing and also take seriously the difficulties encountered by some states in strengthening that portion of GCS that falls within their territory.

Furthermore, international actors need to take into account the plight of the weak members of the society of states to ensure that they can carry out their ethical function, which is to alleviate the shortcomings of civil society in their areas. We shall consider what measures might achieve these outcomes later.

UNDERSTANDING TORTURE IN INTERNATIONAL RELATIONS

Finally, let us see how constitutive theory can help us achieve a better understanding of torture as a problem in contemporary international relations. Involved, as we are, in the so-called 'War on Global Terror' we are often called upon to understand the use of torture as a necessary instrument to be used in defending key ethical values. Here, once again, it often seems as if we have a choice between a concern for the individual rights of suspected terrorists and a concern with the well-being of sovereign states in the system of states. The problem emerges dramatically in those cases where a suspect is to be tortured in order to glean information about a terrorist network and impending attacks. In framing the case for torture the 'ticking bomb' metaphor is often used. This suggests that getting information from a suspect quickly is a precondition for preventing great harm to many people. In making the case for the use of torture (sometimes referred to euphemistically as 'harsh interrogation methods'), the starting point is always that torture is not normally justified from an ethical point of view but that, in exceptional circumstances, it might be. Those making this case almost always argue that the case in hand is indeed an exceptional one.

The justifications for overriding the normal ethical and legal constraints on the use of torture rely on one or more of the following arguments: That the right of the suspect not to be tortured has to be weighed in the balance against the rights of the many who will be harmed were the terrorist act to be carried out; that the harm done to the individual has to be put against the possible harm to the many; that on purely utilitarian grounds overall utility will be maximized by using torture on the suspect and by avoiding the disutility of the terrorist act. On this view what is sought is to maximize the utility for the population as a whole. All of these are versions of the same calculation, that the harm to the one has to be measured against the harm to the many.

There are several standard problems with this way of framing the matter. First, the calculation only works if it is positively known that the suspected terrorist, alone or with others, is indeed planning and able to inflict 'the great harm' mentioned in the calculus. To torture a person on the mere suspicion that he/she might be about to commit a terrorist act is clearly not ethically justifiable because it might often result in the torture of innocent people. Second, this justificatory calculation would clearly not cover those cases where the inquiry is concerned to find out whether the person under interrogation is part of a 'terrorist' network or not. Here again the problem is that interrogations at this stage would still often end up harming innocent individuals. This would happen in all those cases where what was suspected was not indeed the case. The harm inflicted on the individual would not be some slight harm but a really fundamental one that might reduce the person to a life-long psychological wreck. Third, it is now known that when extreme forms of torture are used it is possible to force people to admit to almost anything demanded by the interrogator. It follows then that information extracted will regularly be bad information and as a consequence will not necessarily be the reliable piece of data that would enable the terrorist project to be halted. Fourth, the metaphor of the ticking bomb always assumes that the suspect has the one piece of information that, once known, would enable the clock to be stopped. In any complex social operation, such as a terrorist one, it is seldom the case that the information held by one person would be sufficient, if known, to halt the whole process. Such actions usually involve many actors. It follows, then, that preventing the outrage would thus require data from many sources. It might thus require the torture of many suspects, many of whom might be innocent and many of these under pressure might give unreliable information.

Although I am convinced by the arguments against torture presented above, there is yet a more powerful one to be made by using constitutive theory. Applying the theory to the kind of torture cases that have emerged in recent times, once again shows how constitutive theory can generate richer understandings of contemporary international relations than those which show us as standing before a radical choice between individual rights and states' rights.

As we have seen above, constitutive theory makes the strong claim that all people are currently both civilians in global civil society and citizens in the society of sovereign states. Terror suspects themselves enjoy this ethical standing. So, too, do those doing the torture. The torturers and those being tortured are all civilians and citizens. What takes place between the torturer and the tortured are actions open to evaluation by all the members of these two foundational practices. As always, if the actions undertaken do not measure up to the ethical commitments embedded in these practices, then the actor will lose ethical standing. Not only will the particular person doing the torture lose standing but also those above him/her who authorized the actions. These might be the immediate military or police commanders or commanders of the secret services. At a level of authority yet higher than this are the politicians who endorsed policies that included the use of torture. If the acts undertaken cannot be shown to uphold the core values in the constituting practices, then these people, although seemingly distant from the action, will themselves lose standing in the practice.

What is the likelihood that the use of torture can be shown to support the underlying ethical commitments embedded in global civil society and the society of sovereign states? The chances of this are slim because there is a well-established settled norm against torture. The case for torture has to override this norm. Doing this is notoriously difficult as we shall see.

There is a worldwide recognition that torture is normally wrong. There is no significant group of states or group of individuals who make a principled case in favour of torture as a standard routine for getting information from suspected wrongdoers. There are no plaudits and prizes for outstanding torturers in the way that there are for outstanding judges, generals and members of the police. The general ethical commitment against torture is embodied in most domestic legal systems, in international law and, in particular, in the *United Nations Convention against Torture and Other Cruel, Inhuman or Degrading Treatment or Punishment* which has been signed by 151 states and ratified by 142. There are, of course, many states within which the torture of suspects does take place, but this is almost always done clandestinely and no state openly defends the practice in the international public arena. That it is done secretly is an indication of the existence of the general norm as described. In short, there is a settled norm that torture is wrong. The efforts by the United States government in recent times to define precisely what is to count as torture and what is not torture is itself evidence of the existence of the norm against torture.

Further evidence of this norm is provided by the fact that, generally speaking, those using these methods attempt to keep them secret. The interrogations are carried out in special places far removed from the public eye. An obvious reason for this is that those doing the torturing know that they are infringing a widely held norm. As far as possible those who used these means try to prevent the publication of what they are doing. Not only do they go to lengths to keep what they do from the public eye but they also seek to find means of torture that leave little physical trace on the bodies of those to whom it has been administered. They seek to minimize the physical evidence. This is presumably why the method of 'water boarding' is so popular. This involves subjecting the victim to a procedure that almost drowns him/her. It is terrifying. However, once the victim is revived (brought back from the brink of drowning) there is no evidence on the body that the method was used.

That those using methods of torture in conducting interrogations almost always seek to do it under the cloak of secrecy is incontrovertible. It is prima facie evidence that the actors in question are not confident that the use of this method will be widely interpreted as upholding the norms on which the practices are built. Why is it so difficult to present torture in a positive light?

The answer to this question will become apparent if we turn again to the major argument that is used in justification of the procedure, that, although torture is normally ethically (and legally) unjustifiable, in specific cases an exception has to be made. Here reference is made to one or more of the following features of the situation confronting those about to use the method: that a bomb is ticking and thousands may be wounded or killed; that global terrorism poses an enormous and unusual threat to all that we are and all that we stand for; that the people being dealt with are 'evil' in such a fundamental way that all methods may be used to combat their activities and so on. What are we to make of these claims?

The most important thing to say is that the mere making of such a claim is not a performative act that establishes its truth. Simply because military commanders, the police or intelligence agencies make the claim that the circumstances are exceptional does not establish that they are so. Once the claim has been made it is always open to scrutiny. It can be examined at the time of its making and for years to come. Consider the justification for torture that refers to a ticking bomb – the claim that the information to be extracted from this suspect will prevent an imminent explosion that will harm many. We have to understand this justification as being offered to all citizens and civilians everywhere. Under what conditions, if any, would we as civilians and citizens accept such a justification? When would we say that such a claim was even plausible? Clearly, it would only be plausible in those circumstances where it was known with great certainty that the bomb was in place, that it would definitely go off unless the interrogator got the specific piece of information that it was known that this person about to be tortured had. It would also have to be the case that the interrogator knew of no other way of preventing the bomb exploding. It clearly would not be justifiable to torture a suspect if the information was easily available from some other source not requiring torture. The chances of the authorities having this kind of information seem slim. That it was only one person and one piece of information that was missing would presuppose that the authorities had precise information about the rest of the operation. If they knew about all the other details, then it is highly unlikely that this single person would have the remaining detail that would prevent the whole operation going ahead. In the circumstances in which torture is often used the initial body of knowledge is not at all as precise as the 'ticking bomb' metaphor suggests. The circumstances of the inquiry are far more chaotic. What the agencies face are a set of circumstances in which they are trying to piece together a whole set of fragments of information in order to establish whether there is a plan to place a bomb, hijack a plane or commit some other violent deed. In other words, what is being sought is not a single piece of information but many. Once the net is thrown wider in this way it becomes ever more likely that innocent people will be brought in for interrogation under torture. Indeed, the inquiries might show that, in spite of the initial fears about an impending attack, an attack is not imminent at all. What we see here is that the 'exception' is not nearly as carefully stipulated as one might think. This lack of precision is devastating for the argument from the exception.

Any argument for overriding a widely held ethical norm on the ground that the circumstances are exceptional is only plausible insofar as the exceptional circumstances can be specifically defined. For the argument to work it must be clear to the audience to whom it is addressed what the limits of the exception are. This can be demonstrated as follows: If telling the truth is a widely accepted ethical value, then if someone wishes to justify lying under exceptional circumstances, he/she would have to specify rather narrowly what these might be. A failure to do this would undermine the original principle. If anything at all can count as an exception to the truth-telling principle, then the principle does not count for anything. The general point here is that arguments from the exception always seek to confirm the core principle; they can only do this if the criteria for making an exception are very narrowly specified. As we have seen above, this is very difficult to do.

At the heart of constitutive theory is the notion that actors have to maintain their ethical standing in the practices within which they are constituted as actors. Actors who make the case for the use of torture relying on the argument from the exception will always find it very difficult to specify the precise conditions of the exception. This failure will open them to the countercharge that they are not upholding the core principle behind the exception. In particular, it will open them to the charge that they are not upholding the freedom and diversity that GCS and SOSS make possible. They themselves will come to be seen as the enemy of these practices.

Similarly, if it can be shown that the torturers were not using the method to extract information in exceptional circumstances that were carefully defined, but were using the method to terrorize a whole population, then once again the use of the method will have resulted in the loss of standing and power by the torturer and the gain by those opposing the method.

THE SECURITY OF ANARCHIES: THREATS AND DEFENCES

In what went before we saw how an ethics-centred approach to the analysis of international relations can throw light on a number of different phenomena in international relations. We have considered its application to foreign policy assessment (using the Baker Hamilton Report as an illustration), rival interpretations of private military companies and their role in international relations; humanitarian intervention; illegal migration; the phenomenon of globalization; and the role of torture in international relations. At each point this kind of analysis locates the actions being looked at in their relevant global practices. The approach is holist. I aimed to demonstrate how, in each case, the supporting ethical theory which justifies the anarchical practices seen as a social whole could be used to produce richer interpretations of specific acts, policies and institutions. I now want to show how this approach to international relations can help us understand the strengths and weaknesses of the global anarchies themselves – how it can help us better understand how anarchies, as social institutions, defend themselves.

In the normal course of events anarchies are defended by the individual, self-regarding actions of the actors constituted in them. It is a feature of anarchical societies that each actor in the anarchical society is charged with the duty of self-defence. This applies both in global civil society where, ultimately, individuals have to defend themselves, and also in the society of sovereign states where, at the end of the day, individual sovereign states are responsible for their own self-defence. In pursuit of security, individual actors may make any number of different kinds of plans. Some may fortify themselves and seek to carry the best weaponry, others may form alliances with fellow actors and others still may put in place special forms of defensive organization. When an individual actor in an anarchical society engages in defensive action, although that actor might simply regard his action as being self-regarding, in fact, the act of defence contributes to the defence of the whole. Consider the case of a self-defensive act in civil society. Here, when a rights holder defends his/her rights, this action iterates the values implicit in the overall practice and also contributes to the defence of that portion of civil society in which the actor is located. Similarly, when a state defends itself against attacks on its sovereignty, the very act of self-defence is an iteration of a core value in the anarchical society of states and also helps protect that portion of the society of states that is under threat. In order to make the above more concrete, consider the case of those states that reacted against Iraq's invasion of Kuwait in 1990. By acting to defend that sovereign state, these states were contributing to the security of the whole society of states.

This way of defending the whole by relying on the self-defensive actions of the parts has a lot to be said for it. First, it creates a highly successful motivational structure amongst the participants. The self-interest of the constituent actors drives the defence of the anarchy as a whole. Altruism is not called for. Second, it creates a general and ongoing stance of preparedness amongst the participant actors. Each participant knows that early preparation for defence is likely to prevent attack and to cut down the costs of defence. The default position is that participants know that they cannot rely on a third party for protection so they need to be prepared. Third, it pushes the participating actors towards forming co-operative arrangements with other actors in order to share the costs of self-defence. Fourth, it allows for experimentation amongst the actors with an eye to finding the best modes of defence. Fifth, through a hidden hand process, the number of parties that get engaged in defence is likely to be precisely the number needed. For actors will be loath to expend effort (and incur expenses) beyond that which is needed. Their self-interest will be directed towards limiting costs. There will be in-built incentives to make sure that there is no waste of effort in this endeavour.

In spite of the strengths of the normal mode of self-defence in anarchical societies, these cannot cope with all the threats to such social practices. In particular, there is a kind of threat to an anarchical society which not only affects the participants at whom it is directed but must be understood as a threat to the anarchical society as a whole. In this section I wish to consider the most prominent contemporary version of this kind of threat – that posed to both anarchical societies by what has come to be called 'global terror'. The essence of this kind of threat is to be found in certain actions which are directed towards inducing the members to launch a set of supposedly 'defensive' policies that turn out to be destructive of the very institutional arrangements within which liberty is constituted. Only an ethics-based approach to the understanding of international affairs can fully explain this kind of threat. The next chapter sets out how an ethics-centred approach does this.

4

GLOBAL TERRORISM UNDERSTOOD IN ETHICAL TERMS

The global practice of double anarchy, by definition, includes within itself most people wherever they happen to be. There is no significant group outside of these practices. This is what it means to be 'global'. A logical consequence of this is that any threat to the practice as a whole must be an internal one – it must be a threat that arises from actors who are themselves participants in the practice. Given then that 'terrorists' do not form an identifiable group external to the global practice, the threat cannot take on the form of a conflict between us and them.[1] In their day-to-day lives the so-called terrorists are like us, both civilians and citizens.[2] The phenomenon of global terror poses just such a threat – it is a threat posed by people

[1] I use scare quotes around the word terrorist here to indicate that I am aware of the difficulties associated with the word. In particular, I am aware of the adage that 'one person's terrorist is another's freedom fighter'. However, in what follows I shall simply refer to terrorists without using quotation marks in each case.

[2] This was, indeed, the case with the individuals who launched the attacks on 9/11/2001. Prior to committing their acts of terror, Atta and his associates were civilians and citizens in good standing in the global practices. They claimed the standard sets of rights for themselves and from what one can gather in their day-to-day behaviour respected the civilian and citizenship rights of others. They studied, travelled about, attended air schools and so on. They did not comport themselves as identifiable enemies of civilians and citizens.

other terrorists,
or non-terrorist

who are insiders to our global social practices. These insiders threaten to precipitate a process whereby the other participants in these anarchies set about dismantling and destroying the very structures within which their freedom is constituted. How do terrorists set about doing this?

On the face of the matter, global terrorists, such as the people who launched the attacks on New York, Madrid and London, pose no major threat to the participants in either anarchical society. If we accept for the moment that these attacks were launched by Al Qaeda (AQ), then, given the limited number of people in this organization, the limited hardware available to them and, most importantly, the formidable arsenal of defences ranged against them, it is clear that AQ poses no fundamental threat to either global civil society or the society of sovereign states. Consider the attack that resulted in the destruction of the World Trade Center. Although it was a human tragedy and although it was the result of what was clearly a criminal act, judged both by domestic and by international law, yet, by no stretch of the imagination did it pose a threat to the USA as a sovereign state, nor to the society of sovereign states as a whole. It also did not pose a threat to global civil society seen as a whole. Furthermore, those individual actions by the terrorists (and the ones that came afterwards, in Madrid and London) did not (and are not likely to) spark the emergence of a global mass movement that would threaten the society of states or civil society. In short, Al Qaeda is not a threat in the same league as that which was posed to the international order by national-socialism, fascism or communism in the previous century. It is also not plausible to suppose that this small group could be the catalyst that would bring about a global mass mobilization of Islamic people. There is very little evidence that the bulk of Islamic people currently want, or are moving towards, a view that the international system of states should be destroyed or that global civil society should be replaced with an alternative set of institutional arrangements. Most Islamic people are civilians and citizens in good standing. Islamic scholars (unlike the communist scholars during the Cold War) have not been producing, arguing about and disseminating alternative blueprints about new world orders.[3]

The attacks posed no threat to GCS/SOS. I'm not sure. Symbolic threat?

3 The exception are those few who are currently arguing in the public domain for the establishment of a caliphate. But it is far from clear what this would entail. Is a

If I am correct in asserting that the terrorists pose no immediate and plausible threat to the contemporary structures of world politics, why then is the current spate of terrorist attacks perceived as a major threat to our existing order? Why has it been construed as a threat so great that, in response to it, a war on global terror has been mounted? In what does the threat consist? How is it that so few can be construed as being so dangerous to so many?

An ethics-centred approach explains how the terrorists do this. At the heart of this approach, as we have seen, is the insight that the key actors must be understood in the context of the two anarchies in which they are constituted as such.[4] Each actor, in order to maintain standing as an international actor must obey (and must be seen to obey) the ethical constraints embedded in the relevant global practices. A failure to do this would result in, at the limit, excommunication from the relevant practice. With this in mind, let us now return to the analysis of the phenomenon of global terrorism.

At first glance it may seem as if terrorists who martyr themselves are, by that deed (and by the religious justifications that are offered in support of that deed), clearly indicating to the international public that they are rejecting the existing global social practices in their totality – that they do not see themselves as participants in the

caliphate to be something like a sovereign state that would have state-like status within the existing system of sovereign states? Or, is a caliphatic system to be a completely different kind of international order? There do not appear to be widely accepted answers to these questions. The contrast here is with the set of ideas that pertained during the Cold War which opposed the liberal democratic paradigm. During this period Marxist-Leninists had detailed proposals for what would replace the capitalist order which itself supported the system of sovereign states.

4 It is necessary to stress here that the focus must be on the relevant international practices, not on local social formations which, although they may be important for individual men and women, are not key to understanding their engagement in international affairs. Thus, although the local nations, ethnic groups, religions (and so on) to which individuals belong are no doubt important to them, from the point of view of understanding international affairs they are normally of little relevance. The point being made here is analogous to the following one: That a particular football player is a devout Muslim is of no relevance to whether or not the player is in good standing within the practice of playing football. The criteria which determine who is a player in good standing in the game pay no attention to the personal religious convictions of the players. No doubt religious convictions are of great relevance to some players' lives, but these are of no concern to the rules of the game.

global social practices we have described, but that on the contrary they are completely opposed to these social formations. It may seem as if by that performative they are declaring themselves outsiders. However, this interpretation, let us call it a rejectionist interpretation, although it might describe the individual motivations of some of the actors involved, does not at all capture the significance of their acts as international acts and it certainly does nothing to indicate why their actions are considered a major threat internationally. Imagine some small group of people, let us call them 'the fanatics', who, on some reading of an old testament text, turn themselves into human bombs, commit suicide and in doing so kill many innocent people. Would such deeds, no doubt dreadful in themselves, pose a major threat to global civil society or to the society of states in any conventional sense of the word? I suggest that such acts would pose no more of a threat to our global practices than that posed to international order by those individual school children (and university students) who, from time to time, go on killing sprees in schools and universities. What they do is terrible and reprehensible, but it does not threaten the existing order in any fundamental way. The threat to our international arrangements posed by the terrorist martyrs (or by the fanatics as I have described them) does not lie in the material damage they do (or the damage that they can threaten to do). It cannot be this for there are too few of them, too thinly dispersed globally, to move beyond spectacle, towards the destruction (or defeat) of whole states or whole societies. Nor does it lie in the threat of escalation (the recruitment of thousands of martyrs), who would deploy worldwide and wreak sufficient damage to bring GCS and the society of sovereign states to the brink of collapse. There is no evidence of such a large-scale mobilization in international affairs as we know it today. Most people wherever they happen to be are active participants in the society of sovereign states and in global civil society. They show every indication of wanting to remain so.

There is an alternative interpretation of the global terror used by AQ which might initially seem quite strong, but which on closer scrutiny is also not convincing. According to this we ought to interpret AQ's campaign solely in terms of the religious canons of Islam as set out in the Koran and the Haditha. Such an understanding would make the case that AQ is engaged in a Jihad – a holy war. A full understanding of Jihad would, of course, require that we enter into the ongoing debate taking place amongst Islamic scholars about the precise meaning of this concept. Although such thoroughgoing religious interpretations can and have been given and, although this kind of interpretation (a Jihadist one) is, no doubt, important to many individual members of AQ in that it provides them with the motivation to do what they do, the interpretation is still weak when looked at in the context of our global practices seen in the round. To read AQ's campaign in this way is to see it simply as attempting to set up a conflict between the followers of Islam and the rest. This is to understand it in conventional terms of a war between 'us' and 'them'. Here again, this explanation does not explain why AQ is seen as a major threat, even by, or especially by, the only superpower and its allies. This interpretation fails because it is simply implausible to suppose that AQ is itself launching, or could launch, a campaign in which all or most Islamic people worked together to bring about an end to global civil society and the society of sovereign states. It is implausible because most Islamic people, while being good followers of Islam, are simultaneously active civilians in good standing in global civil society and are citizens in good standing who actively participate in the society of sovereign states. There is no widespread rejection of these practices by those of the Islamic faith. Thus, it is implausible to suppose that they are forming themselves into a cohesive group opposed to the existing global institutions in their totality.

The two interpretations discussed above fail for the reasons given, but they also fail because they do not account for the ways in which AQ is a 'player' in the international practices of our time. An ethics-centred approach such as constitutive theory presents us with a more convincing account of the path that has taken AQ from insignificant international actor to a major player in international affairs. According to the model presented in this book, we can best understand AQ's global power in terms of the 'moves' it has made within the global practice of double anarchy. My central claim is that, in what AQ has done and in what it continues to do in the international context, it seeks to present what it does as ethical in terms of well-known values embedded in the two anarchies we have been studying. It displays a sophisticated understanding of the 'rules of the international ethical game' and it has scored significant ethical victories in this 'game'. After a weak set of opening moves, it has quite rapidly scored some significant gains in the international practices.

There are many different planks to the platform of arguments AQ uses to present its case to the international community. The arguments are to be found in tapes made of speeches by Osama Bin Laden and other AQ leaders that are broadcast by Al Jazeera and then re-broadcast around the world.[5] They are also to be found in what captured members of AQ have said and in what Islamic religious leaders have said. The arguments are often not presented in a systematic and compact form, but taken together they may be read as making an ethical case addressed to the core values held by civilians and citizens of sovereign states. In studying how AQ has been active in GCS and the system of sovereign states, we need to keep in mind that the conflict is ongoing and AQ has built up its case during several phases. Using a boxing metaphor we might refer to the phases of the struggle as 'rounds' in a fight.

In round one, AQ attempted to make use of the standard ethical norms of international conduct, but overall it acquitted itself poorly. AQ presented itself as fighting a war against the imperial aggression of the USA and its allies in the Middle East. The case made was an exceptionally weak one. Consider its claim to be fighting a war. The notion of war might have specific connotations within Islam, but these need not detain us here.[6] What is of concern here is the notion of war as a legitimate act within the anarchical society of sovereign states. As things currently stand the major settled norm in the practice of states which justifies going to war is the one which justifies war in response to aggression. From the outset AQ has appealed to this norm in a number of different ways. In the immediate aftermath of the attack on the twin towers AQ claimed that the USA and its allies were indirectly guilty of supporting aggression through offering support to Israel against the Palestinians. At that time this was a weak claim. For although it might have found favour with its own followers and with the Palestinians, this was a weak claim within the

---

5 A particularly lucid spokesperson of AQ is Adam Yehiye Gada, some of whose speeches can be found in the public domain on www.youtube.com.

6 They need not concern us for Islam is not a global practice in the sense that it is not a practice within which everyone is a participant. Global civil society and the society of sovereign states are the only global practices in this sense.

context of the global practices for a number of reasons: The Palestinian people have aspirations to become a sovereign state; indeed, they may have a good ethical claim to statehood, but as things stand they do not constitute a state. So strictly speaking Israel cannot be held guilty of aggression against a 'state' of Palestine, for no such state exists. So the initial claim by AQ to be fighting a war against an aggressor was a tenuous one. It was tenuous for another reason as well. AQ is not itself a state. Within the global practice of states only legitimate authorities, states, have the right to make war. So AQ's initial claim to the ethical high ground when launching its attack on the USA, while it may have been strong on Islamic grounds and carried conviction in local Middle Eastern political circles, was weak in terms of the norms embedded in the system of sovereign states. At the moment of the attack on the USA on 9/11/2001 the ethical standing of AQ as an actor in international relations was, then, extremely weak. The nature of its acts decreased its minimal standing even more. Its actions and statements offended the basic human rights norms that civilians enjoy in global civil society and its actions did not gain any support whatsoever from the norms governing the conduct of war within the practice of states.

The initial international reactions to AQ's acts on 9/11/2001, which were almost universally critical, strongly endorsed the interpretation offered above, that AQ enjoyed little or no moral standing in international affairs at that time and that what it had done was ethically obnoxious. It was, from the point of view of the participants in global civil society and the society of sovereign states, an outlaw actor that did things that were both illegal and ethically wrong.

No doubt, AQ's ethical standing would have remained that way had the international community reacted to the attacks by branding the perpetrators as criminals both in domestic and international law terms. If the international community, led by the USA, had done this and had devised policies to follow this judgement, then AQ would have had to rely solely on its Islamic credentials which justified its action with reference to Jihad. As some already mentioned, while such justifications might carry weight in Islamic circles, they do not carry weight within the two major international practices. If such a policy of branding the terrorists as criminals had been followed then terrorists, who were subsequently apprehended, would have been tried and sentenced as criminals. In the face of wide condemnation of

AQ actors as criminals it would have been difficult for the organization to recruit martyrs and to mobilize political and emotional support, except amongst the most extreme supporters of Islam. It would have been difficult, because the vast bulk of Islamic people worldwide are not opposed to the society of states and to the rules of civil society. Indeed, not only are they not opposed to these anarchical systems but they are active participants in them and can be expected to uphold (and indeed do uphold) the detailed prescriptions within these practices. Most Islamic people are good civilians and good citizens. In opposing such criminality, most people worldwide, in their capacities as both civilians and citizens, would have been able to call on the ethical foundations which ground the institutions in which these statuses are located, in order to condemn the criminal behaviour of AQ operatives and to take appropriate action against them.

In the event, however, and rather dramatically, the response of the USA and its allies was not to identify the terrorist acts as 'criminal' but to label them 'acts of war'. Having done this the USA and its allies then went to 'war against terror'. As is well known, they used military force to attack and effect regime change in Afghanistan and then in Iraq. The consequences of this labelling and the acts that followed were, from an ethics-centred understanding of world politics, very dramatic indeed. By declaring the campaign a 'war on terror' the USA and its coalition partners effectively cast AQ as the other party in a war. This immediately gave some credibility to AQ's claim to be making war. For if war was being made against it, then it could quite properly claim that it itself was engaged in a war. But what justification could it provide for fighting a war? After the military campaigns against Afghanistan and Iraq, AQ could claim to be fighting aggression by the USA and its allies against these two sovereign states. Where earlier, prior to 9/11, its case had been weak, it now appeared much stronger. For Afghanistan and Iraq, both sovereign states, had been occupied by foreign states and regime change had been effected. AQ could now claim, with much more plausibility than before, that it was fighting international aggression against sovereign states. It could claim that it was fighting illegal occupation and imperialism. It could now point to the fact that here was the world's only superpower and its allies, with massive military might at their disposal, occupying sovereign independent states. So, ironically, where prior to 9/11 AQ's claim to be fighting a war against USA aggression was weak, it was now much stronger.

At the same time the actions of the Israeli government further strengthened the ethical case made by AQ and the insurgent groups who support it. By the Israeli government's refusal to co-operate with Hamas, the winner of the elections for a Palestinian authority, and by its instituting draconian measures against Palestine, includ-ing military action, it became easy for AQ to portray Israel as acting contrary to the norms embedded in the anarchical society of states. A key norm in this practice is one that accords autonomy to sovereign states. Within the international system of states there is widespread agreement that there ought to be an independent Palestinian state. Building on this agreement, it thus now became easy for AQ to claim that this norm was being flouted by Israel and that the USA in supporting Israel was guilty of supporting aggression. Similarly, if the events in Israel/Palestine are examined from the point of view of the values implicit in civil society, then, here too, it is apparent that by denying people their civil liberties Israel is posing a threat to that portion of global civil society – it is threatening human rights.

In seeking to justify its actions in the current war, AQ has been able to add yet another plank to its platform by pointing to the injustices perpetrated by the USA and its allies in the way that the war has been conducted (sometimes referred to as the *ius in bello*). Here again it has been able to appeal to very standard just war criteria current in the society of states. The treatment of illegal combatants, the use of torture in the interrogation of prisoners, the killing of civilians in the conduct of military operations and the wholesale destruction of private civilian property, all strengthen the ethical case of AQ and its allied groups to be conducting a just war. Again I must stress that the case it is now able to make does not depend on appeals to Islamic values (although it still makes use of these to appeal to its own supporters) but it rests on values implicit in the global practices within which we are all constituted as civilians and citizens.

In summary, then, we have outlined how the initially very weak justification for AQ's acts of terror have been made much stronger by the subsequent interpretation put on them by the USA and its allies and by the responses that were instituted as a result of that interpretation. By calling what was done 'war' and by launching what was deemed a 'just war' in response, the ethical landscape has been drastically changed in AQ's' favour. Where at the earlier stage it seemed reasonable to assert there were very few people willing to join, follow or endorse the course of action set out by AQ, in the light of subsequent reactions by the USA and its allies, there are now many people worldwide who, in their capacities as civilians and citizens, are prepared to either tacitly support the action against USA occupation or actively to become involved in opposing it. There is also a very large group of people *within* the coalition (for example USA and British citizens) who are radically opposed to ongoing military engagement in these two states. This internal opposition has weakened the authority of these states in the eyes of the international community of states.

What I wish to highlight at this point is how important it is to understand the thrust and counterthrusts in this conflict in terms of the manoeuvres the parties make to secure for themselves the ethical high ground within the edifice of the double anarchy. What matters for all people engaged in this set of actions and reactions is making the ethical assessments about what has been done, what ought to be done and what is being done in the region. The analysis just given indicates the dire consequences that follow from basing one's policies and actions on mistaken ethical assessments. In spite of all the financial and military muscle at their disposal the superpower and its allies find that, in the present conflict, they are now very much on the defensive. This has come about, I would argue, through a failure properly to understand the complex ethical dimensions of international politics. Traditional forms of analysis in international relations do not adequately get to grips with the all important ethical dimensions of international affairs.

We saw in the previous discussion how the threat posed by AQ has grown as a result of the reactions that it managed to elicit from the targets of its attacks. These reactions, when read through the prism of the ethical values embedded in the double anarchy, weakened the ethical standing of the victims of the terrorist attacks and strengthened the ethical standing of the perpetrators.

The threat posed to the double anarchy by AQ and international terrorism is even greater than the analysis so far has suggested. As mentioned earlier, there is another set of reactions that AQ's attacks have brought forth that is even more threatening to the long-term well-being of our global practices. I refer here to those actions that call for policies that restrict, undermine or do away with the very liberties (and the possibilities for pluralism that they make possible) that are the raison d'être of the anarchical practices in the first place. There are some policies that have been put forward and put into practice in response to terrorist attacks which threaten to destroy the two practices in question much more effectively than the dramatic attacks launched by the terrorists could ever have done (or could ever do). What we are examining here is how acts of terrorism can bring forth responses from the targets of those attacks that cause them to start a process of self-destruction. Let us consider the road to self-destruction in each anarchical society in turn.

THE THREAT OF SELF-DESTRUCTION IN CIVIL SOCIETY

Global civil society, as we have seen, consists of the society of people who recognize one another as the holders of first-generation rights (the so called 'negative liberties'). This society of rights holders is corroded when any member or group of members refuses to recognize the rights of fellow civilians or sets about abusing those rights. A threat by a single individual to a single individual, of course, does not do much damage to civil society as a whole, but a threat by many to many does. The key underlying values of this social institution are that it makes possible a certain kind of freedom and that it makes possible the co-existence of a great diversity of life projects (it allows different rights holders to pursue lives based on very divergent ideas of the good, be they Christian, Islamic, Buddhist, Hindu, secular, socialist or communist). If, in response to terrorist attacks, civilians (individually or as a group) start 'protecting' themselves in ways that flout (or repudiate) the basic rules of civil society, then they are ironically in some sense acting in ways that are complicit with the terrorists in damaging the edifice within which they are constituted as free in the first place. Here is an example of how this might come about.

Terrorist attacks, by definition, infringe civilian rights to safety of the person. Consider the case of Anthony Fatyi-Williams who was killed by a terrorist who blew himself up on a bus in central London on 7th July 2005. Beyond being a tragedy for the family, this was a deed of significance for civil society as a whole. The bomber had shown utter disrespect for the rights of his victims on the bus. Furthermore, since the targeting of the attack appeared quite arbitrary, the threat extended to civilians in London and other cities around the world. In the aftermath of such a terrorist attack and when faced with the threat of more attacks, civilians in global civil society typically, and quite justifiably, become preoccupied with security. What kinds of actions have civilians undertaken and which of these may be seen as legitimate and which of them threaten the very society they are supposed to be securing?

In seeking to protect their own rights, civilians are entitled to identify those who pose a threat, to undertake steps to prevent the threat materializing and to punish those who abuse their rights. All of these are subject to the constraint, that in doing these things, civilians do not abuse the rights of others. In doing these things the actors reinforce the core norms of the practice. The norms are consolidated by being reiterated.

Let us start by considering a list of ethically unproblematic manoeuvres civilians might make to secure their rights in the face of global terror and then move on to consider some more problematic ones. At a personal level civilians might move to parts of the world where terrorist acts are rare. They may take a range of precautions to prevent themselves falling victim to terror attacks. These might include avoiding certain forms of transport, bypassing certain localities or instituting security regimes while travelling, while at home and at work. Also, they might mandate their governments to pass legislation making terrorism more difficult. Thinking of the society more widely civilians might engage with attempts to deal with the social conditions which give rise to terrorism in the first place. A first step in this direction could be giving support to research into the causes and origins of terrorism. If these are found to be political repression, underdevelopment, lack of education, lack of market opportunities and so on, then, of course, attempts to alleviate these would be in order. All of the above-mentioned causes of terrorism could be framed in terms of a denial of rights to the people from whose ranks the terrorists arise. It follows then that, in order to avoid terrorism, civilians ought to orient themselves to making civil society rights real for everyone everywhere. There is a huge literature on what might broadly be termed 'development' and on what needs to be done in order to create a vibrant global civil society of rights holders. The literature reveals that there are difficult and ongoing disputes within this area of inquiry. I cannot delve into these now.[7] Here, once again, all of these actions are endorsements of the fundamental norms of this practice.

In contrast to the actions that nurture civil society discussed above, I now wish to discuss some of the supposedly defensive actions that civilians might take in response to terror that might turn out to be destructive of civil society. Such destructive acts are those which undermine the ethical relationships of mutual recognition between civilians: those that undermine the settled norms of the practice. For example, terrorist acts bring about a self-destructive motion in civil society when they cause civilians to regard and act towards other civilians, not as rights holders but as potential threats, because of some or other general characteristic such as, for example, the fact that they are Black, are from Africa, are followers of Islam or are simply foreigners. The destructive moment happens when, because some so-called 'terrorists' originated from within this (Black/African/Islamic/foreign) group, it is then presumed that the whole group is filled with potential terrorists and the freedoms of the whole group are curtailed.[8] When civilians treat the members of a whole group (however defined) as wrongdoers because of the wrongdoing of a few in that group, then, by making an error in logic, they commit an ethical wrong. Their action, were it to become widespread, would destroy civil society. It is a primary feature of civil society that in it a key ethical value for civilians is that they regard one another primarily as rights holders and not as members of this or that religious, ethnic, or racial group. A particularly good example of this destructive action happens when civilians in a given area start regarding foreigners not as civilians from elsewhere but as people who are likely to become criminals and terrorists here where they are. The destructive moment occurs when, on account of this judgement, they then refuse to trade with them, employ them, play with them, have their children in the same schools as their children, live

7 For articles on policies designed to deal with development see the journal *Development Policy Review* (Blackwell).

8 This is the fallacy of generalizing from small numbers. That three terrorists were Black does not entail that all Blacks are terrorists. It is also not plausible to argue that because most terrorists are followers of Islam it is probable that most future terrorists will be, too. The numbers are too small to ascertain such probabilities.

near them and so on. Where the drive to security achieves this result what has been achieved is the destruction of a portion of civil society. The society that comes into being as a result of these actions is no longer a civil society.

The point being made above not only applies locally but also applies on the global stage. If, in response to an attack by a few Islamic terrorists on some civilians in one place, many civilians then refuse to do all of the above things with Islamic people in many other places around the world, then, once again, those doing the refusing are undermining civil society. They themselves are guilty of ethical wrongdoing insofar as they are complicit in destroying the civil society within which they are constituted as free civilians. Thus, when civilians, let us say, in France band together to prevent civilians from Africa coming to France, moving about there, seeking friends, partners, fellow religionists and jobs there, then those French people doing this are contributing to the destruction of a portion of global civil society (of that portion that falls within French territory). The hypothetical example refers to France, but, in fact, in the wake of the terrorism we have witnessed, there are many instances of the rise of party political positions similar to that just described.

Let me restate the point made in the previous paragraph. Were a few acts of terrorism to have the effect of getting civilians to act in civil society destroying ways that erode its core norms, then the terrorists would have achieved the multiplier effect that is the very engine of terrorist power; they would have succeeded in getting civilians to start destroying key aspects of civil society themselves.

THE THREAT OF SELF-DESTRUCTION IN THE SOCIETY OF SOVEREIGN STATES

Let us now turn to the society of sovereign states. What I am concerned with here is the question: What defensive reactions to terrorism could terrorists precipitate that would result in the society of sovereign states destroying itself?

Earlier we saw how the society of sovereign states may be interpreted as providing remedies to certain ethical shortcomings produced through the working of civil society. The remedies are secured by building on the ethical achievements of civil society and not by replacing it. It follows that self-destructive actions undertaken by citizens who claim to be securing fundamental values would be those actions which *either* undermined the system of mutual recognition in *civil society* that constitutes its core values of freedom and pluralism for rights holders *or* any action that undermined the elaborate system of mutual recognition in the *society of sovereign states* through which the core values of free citizenship and diversity are constituted. There are two different ways in which actions, supposedly in defence of the values embedded in the society of sovereign states, could end up undermining those very values. They need to be distinguished from one another.

First, there are those defensive actions by states which could destroy the social instruments (institutions) through which the society of sovereign states protects civil society. By so doing such actions indirectly undermine the ethical values embedded in civil society. Second, there are those actions which could undermine the ethical values constituted within the society of sovereign states, in particular citizenship and the pluralism it makes possible. Let us look at each of these in turn.

In what ways do states, in the name of self-defence, start destroying the mechanisms that safeguard civilian rights? They do this when they institute security policies in the face of terrorism without building into the policy proposals any of the many safeguards of human rights that have been developed over the centuries. Doing this undermines the existing safeguards. They also do this when they institute policies without proposing any plausible alternatives to the standard safeguards.

Civil society creates a set of actors who are free to pursue their own life plans subject to the constraint that they respect the freedom of other actors in this society. But, as discussed earlier, the interactions of free people over time produce inequalities in social power and social position. As a consequence some civilians suffer an ongoing temptation to use their power and position to advance their own interests while overriding the rights of others. In order to avoid this noxious outcome, civilians have, over time, devised a number of institutional methods to prevent such rights-abusing behaviour. Building these institutions was not done in a neat series of rational actions, but came about over time through a process of trial and error. Briefly, the most successful of these instruments have turned out to be:

- the *separation of power* which has been achieved, inter alia, by dividing the task of protecting global civil society between 193 different sovereign states. Each state is entrusted to protect the rights of civilians in that portion of global civil society that falls within its boundaries.[9] This division of power ensures that a failure to protect rights by one state does not adversely affect all civilians everywhere. The division of the world into sovereign states protects civilian rights by limiting the harm state failure (or state abuse of rights) in one state can achieve on the global stage. The harm is, as it were, quarantined within a specific state's territory.
- the practice of seeking *balances of power* between states ensures that a state or an alliance of states set on abusing civilian rights can be countered by a balancing alliance of states.
- the institution of *the rule of law* both within states and between states. This ensures first that the protection of rights is not left simply to the goodwill of rulers but is built into a constitutional structure and also that there is a process in place whereby 'law regulates its own production' so that there are legal constraints on what powerful rulers and powerful states can do with the law.[10]

Furthermore, built into the rule of law is:

- the principle of *mixed government* such that different people in a polity are given different functions within government in ways that seek to avoid them developing interests that coincide which tempt them into wrongful collusion.
- the principle of *checks and balances* such that one branch of government is overseen and monitored by another (the usual division is between executive, legislative and judicial branches of government).

---

9 That they see themselves as having this duty is indicated by their membership of the UN and endorsement of any number of rights-respecting treaty commitments initiated by the UN. Their commitment to the rights of civil society is also indicated by their participation in the global market, which is a rights-based institution.

10 The rule of law is better developed within states, but it is increasingly being made real within international relations. On law regulating its own creation see Finnis, 1980.

- *democratic accountability* such that the different people in government and the different branches of government are made accountable to the people over whom they are governing. This principle is not yet well entrenched in the international relations between states, although there are signs of this improving.[11]

The techniques civilians have developed for protecting civil society are better developed within constitutional states than they are internationally, but, nevertheless, elements of all of these techniques are to be found at both the domestic and the international level.

In the current war against terror the threat of self-destruction arises when states start following policies that either undermine these devices or fail to put new ones in place. Many states have put in place a whole range of measures that undermine the protective institutional devices just listed. It would require another volume to present a detailed account of the many measures that have been enacted which effectively decommission these devices, but the core point is easily made. The superpower and its allies, together with many other states, have reacted to global terror by instituting a raft of security-related measures that disable or bypass the rights-protecting devices mentioned. By doing this they threaten in fundamental ways the values embedded in civil society and the society of states. These measures include those that give police extra powers to detain and question without the normal human rights safeguards; those that blur the line between police action and military action; those that permit interrogation techniques that severely threaten human rights; those that allow wide latitude to intelligence agencies where no clear rights-protecting oversight is in place; actions that permit those captured in the 'war on terror' to be treated in a way quite different from that guaranteed in international law to prisoners of war; the systems of co-operation between states that have been set up to ferry suspects from one country to another without the normal legal procedures being followed (extraordinary rendition); and many others.[12]

11 See a discussion of the trend towards protection of individuals in international relations and the progress towards recognizing people as having a right to democratic government in Franck, 1999.

12 See the detailed research on the erosion of rights-protecting machinery effected by security measures undertaken in pursuit of the war on terror which is listed by the Challenge Project at http://www.libertysecurity.org/.

In doing these things the governments of states have undertaken measures that, in the name of protecting civil society, are in fact destructive of it. Where this has happened, once again the terrorists have achieved a multiplier effect far beyond what might have been expected from an evaluation of their initial resources. With very little conventional power (economic or military) at its disposal AQ has been highly successful in prodding actors in GCS and in the society of states to engage in self-destructive action. Once states have embarked on this kind of behaviour, then the way is opened for Al Qaeda (and all sorts of other opposition groups) to start pointing to the moral turpitude of the defending states. This pushes the ethical standing of the target states down and that of the oppositional groups up. This is a great source of power and authority for Al Qaeda. It sets in train a series of events that can lead to changes of government, changes of policies and to major re-alignments in international politics.

The power of AQ then lies in its ability to prod participants in the anarchical societies into ethically self-destructive responses, responses that lead them (us) to circumvent the protections of civilian and citizenship rights; and responses that lead them to treat some fellow civilians and citizens as second-class because they come from groups associated with terrorism (Islamic, Black, African) or because they come from weak states from within which terrorists have emerged in the past.

The ethics-centred form of analysis presented here indicates that analyses that simply condemn terrorist acts and then recommend putting in place policies to stop them at all costs do not fully capture the ethical complexities of international relations. It highlights the need ethically to assess the responses to terrorism in order to determine whether they advance, strengthen and consolidate the values implicit in the anarchical societies. If the means used in pursuit of the wrongdoers undermine these, then ironically the terrorists gain by weakening the ethical standing of key actors in international society. This, then, has a direct effect on their political power.

The effect of the ethical self-destructive behaviour described above is to open the way for the emergence of (and for action by) many different groups that may turn out to be radically destructive of GCS and the society of sovereign states. These emerge when civilians and citizens start feeling that their rights are not secure.

They then become vulnerable to approaches by all kinds of political entrepreneurs who seek to mobilize them politically around religious, ethnic, national and other ideologies. We have seen evidence of this phenomenon in many different parts of the world in recent times. In all such cases, the sectional groups gain support from people who are disaffected with the ethical performance of the global anarchies. They find fault with their state within the system of states or they find that their civilian rights are not being respected and protected. These groups can then launch their own 'terrorist' – type attacks at different targets in international system. Typically, the groups, when evaluated in traditional terms, will not be very powerful. However, if they are able to provoke defensive action by the powerful actors that undercut their ethical positions, then they will have, once again, gained considerable political advantage. These groups that start out without much legitimacy may increase their legitimacy when they provoke self-destructive behaviour by members of the liberty-constituting anarchies.

5

DEFENDING ANARCHIES

In the previous chapter I showed how an ethics-centred approach to international relations can bring to light a particularly dangerous form of threat we face in our anarchical global practices. The method displayed terrorists making use of a particular form of ethical leverage available to them in contemporary world politics. We discussed the way in which such groups as AQ can use terrorist-style events to lever civilians, citizens and states into ethically self-destructive responses. In the light of this discussion I now wish to turn to the question: Why is it that our anarchical societies are currently so vulnerable to this kind of provocation to self-destruct? What is it about our contemporary world that allows such small terrorist forces to have such a major global impact? We must have some answers to these questions before we can devise ways in which anarchical societies can defend themselves from such threats.

I would suggest that AQ's success at accumulating support (and thus power) springs from its ability correctly to diagnose a set of ethical problems that beset the contemporary world and to find ways to exploit these. It has identified ethical tensions in our contemporary global order that are the source of acute concern to thousands of millions worldwide. It has calculated that, if it were able to get powerful actors to act in ways that showed these conventionally powerful actors to be insensitive to these burning ethical issues, then the outcome would be a surge of outrage on a global scale against those actors and their ethical failings. This would lead to their losing standing and, as a consequence, power. It would lead to the formation of any number of oppositional movements directed towards opposing the wrongdoers.

Let me be more specific. The terrorist movements such as AQ have tapped into the following vulnerability of contemporary global practices. They have correctly understood that global civil society and the society of sovereign states are particularly vulnerable at the moment because, in the current globalized world, for thousands of millions of people, the rights they enjoy as civilians and citizens are notional rather than real. As things currently stand for many people their statuses as civilians and citizens are formal and hollow. In civil society millions consider themselves to be the holders of a rich set of fundamental liberties, but find that in practice these are under constant threat. Their rights to freedom of speech, association, conscience, academic freedom, safety of the person, the right to own, buy and sell property (and the other individual rights usually included on the list) are often almost entirely aspirational and do not have much real significance in their daily lives. In many places the states within which they find themselves do not protect their civilian rights but actively threaten them. Zimbabwe is but one example of a place where this is happening at the moment. Many other states, particularly in Africa and Asia, are not much better. What is more, all the ethical problems of civil society mentioned earlier, such as those found in the endemic competition, alienation and unequal power found in civil society locally, are now becoming increasingly manifest on a global level. This follows from the global division of labour, high-speed communication and the mobility of the factors of production. Furthermore, they are finding that the ethical solutions to these that were to some extent found within individual states are not working out at the global level. So when movements (many of them at the grass roots) are able, with considerable plausibility, to show that counterterrorist actions undermine these core values, rather than promote them, many people are convinced by these arguments and to some measure withdraw their support from the actors who in the name of opposing terror bring about unethical outcomes.

Similarly, for many people the rights of citizenship, especially the rights of democratic citizenship, are also notional. They find that the states that they live in do not allow them to enjoy the full fruits of these rights. A particular problem they have is that they find that citizenship rights they enjoy do little to alleviate the ethical problems produced by global civil society – unending competition on the global level, alienation on a worldwide scale and global inequalities that seem to be growing worse rather than better.

What many civilians and citizens are finding is that, instead of the society of states being an ethical social formation that solves the ethical problems of global civil society, as things currently stand, the society of states is reinforcing the ethical flaws of global civil society and is heightening the ethical problems experienced in it. Far from providing a resolution to the problems experienced in civil society, the society of states is aggravating them. So, for example, we find that the developed states of the world are seeking to promote the advantage of their portion of civil society, even if this is at the cost of other portions – even if this involves abusing the rights of others. Often this is accompanied by a hypocritical mouthing of free market ideas. States are beginning to act like firms.[1] They are acting as an extension of civil society rather than as a resolver of the ethical tensions found within it.

To repeat the core points: In their self-destructive and often hypocritical responses to terrorism, many states have opened a window of opportunity for civilians and citizens to start articulating their judgement that states are failing to realize the values implicit in the practices within which they are created as international actors. AQ and other groups are able to point to double standards, hypocrisy and self-serving behaviour. AQ is able to present itself as acting on behalf of those many for whom rights are not real. At some future time, the terrorists, who are normally portrayed as amoral and fanatical, may turn out to have been the catalyst that launched a powerful round of internal criticisms by participants in the double anarchy. There would be considerable irony in this. For, if this analysis is correct, global terror, far from being a completely unethical force, may yet prove to have been the trigger to a round of self-examination by the participants in the two anarchies. This examination, if well done, would expose how the ethically maladroit responses of many

1 See on this Stopford & Strange, 1991.

governments to terrorism have opened the way for a set of, what might turn out to be, progressive transformational responses that in the long run will significantly improve the ability of the two practices to live up to their core ethical commitments. For this benign outcome to be achieved, though, requires of us participants in the freedom-creating double anarchy that we correctly understand the ethical context in which we and the terrorists are acting. The present work is an attempt to promote such an understanding.

How then have the anarchies defended themselves from the threat posed to them by this double-barrelled attack, first by AQ directly, then by the self-destructive responses of major powers? In anarchies, as we have seen, every participant is given the task of defending his/her own status as a participant. This is a defining feature of this form of social structure. What we have seen in the current 'war on terror' is how this process works in practice. The first steps in defence were the ethically misguided ones we have discussed. The second wave of defence has been much more ethically sophisticated. In it, many participants, in their capacity as civilians and as citizens worldwide, have reacted with indignation to the measures that were instituted to combat Al Qaeda and global terror generally. In the press, in marches, in social movements, in political parties, in universities, in academic writing, in churches and in many other forums, civilians, who, of course, are also citizens, have roundly condemned the following: the pretexts used for going to war, the lies told at the time, the fabricated intelligence reports, the method used in the war, the interrogation techniques employed, the treatment of combatants, the extraordinary rendition procedures and many other things. They have objected to the erosion of civil liberties within states; they have objected to the denial of national self-determination to groups such as the Palestinians; they have objected to foreign occupation of sovereign states; they have objected to the bypassing of United Nations techniques; they have objected to the double standards; in particular, they have objected to an ostensible commitment to free market principles which are then overridden on narrow nationalist reasons. They have objected to the blocking of the free flow of labour. They have sought to highlight the way in which weak states are kept weak by the actions of the strong. They have highlighted how strong states have failed to commit sufficient resources to the building-up of weak states into viable modern states.

All of these criticisms do not oppose the global practices and the values embedded in them, but rely on appeals to these very values. The number of people involved in these critical activities is enormous compared to the few who were involved in the terrorist acts themselves.

Besides referring to the very specific shortcomings pointed out in the previous paragraph, civilians and citizens everywhere are beginning to comment on a new set of problems. They are noticing how the ethical shortcomings of civil society that were initially experienced within states are now emerging on the global stage. An understanding is emerging that these will require new solutions. The trick will be to craft solutions that do not destroy in the process the ethical solutions already found in the system of states.

The only long-term solution to the threat posed by global terror is to tackle the conditions of possibility that make their actions feasible. Participants in global civil society and the society of states need to take their own values seriously and need to attempt to make them real for everybody everywhere. This is, of course, a mammoth task. It is not something that can be done within individual states alone. It will have to come about through a concerted effort by all of us in our capacities both as civilians and citizens alike.

REFERENCES

Amin, S. (1974). *Accumulation on a world scale*. Hassocks: Harvester Press.

Anderson, M. (1993). *The rise of modern diplomacy 1450–1919*. London: Longman.

Ashley, R. (1987). The geopolitics of geopolitical space: Toward a critical social theory of international politics. *Alternatives, 12*(4), 403–434.

Baker, J. A. I., Hamilton, L. H., *et al.* (2006). *The Iraq Study Group Report* [Bipartisan congressional study group, Congress, USA]. Washington, DC: United States Institute for Peace.

Bayliss, J., & Smith, S. (eds). (2006). *The globalization of world politics (3rd edition)*. Oxford: Oxford University Press.

Beernink, S. (2005). *Report on the private military organisations project* [Report of the Inter-church Council]. Amsterdam: IKR.

Brown, C. (1992). *International relations theory: New normative approaches*. New York: Columbia University Press.

Brownlie, I. (1979). *Principles of public international law*. Oxford: Oxford University Press.

Buchanan, A. (1989). Assessing the communitarian critique of liberalism. *Ethics, 99*, 867.

Bull, H. (1977). *The anarchical society*. London: Macmillan.

Bull, H. (1984). *Intervention in world politics*. Oxford: Oxford University Press.

Buzan, B., Jones, C., & Little, R. (1993). *The logic of anarchy: Neorealism to structural realism*. New York: Columbia University Press.

Christian, O. (2005). *Private military companies in Iraq: A force for good?* Brussels: Challenge Project. (http://www.libertysecurity.org/article127.html).

Cochran, M. (1995). Cosmopolitanism and communitarianism in a post-cold war world. In *Boundaries in question: New directions in international relations* (pp. 40–53). London: Pinter Press.

Cochran, M. (2000). *Normative theory in international relations: A pragmatist approach*. Cambridge: Cambridge University Press.

Crick, B. (1964). *In defence of politics*. Harmondsworth: Penguin.

De Tarczynski, S. (2008). Rights-Australia: 'Pacific solution' for boat people rolled back. *IPS*. (http://ipsnews.net/news.asp?idnews=40583).

Delaney, C. (ed.). (1994). *The liberalism-communitarianism debate: Liberty and community values*. Lanham, MD: Rowman and Littlefield.

Devji, F. (2005). *Landscapes of the Jihad: Militancy morality and modernity*. London: Hurst and Company.

Dunne, T. (1997). Liberalism. In J. Bayliss & S. Smith (eds), *The globalization of international politics*. Oxford: Oxford University Press.

Etzioni, A. (ed.). (1998). *The essential communitarian reader*. Oxford: Oxford University Press.

Finnis, J. (1980). *Natural law and natural rights*. Oxford: Oxford University Press.

Franck, T. M. (1999). *The empowered self: Law and society in the age of individualism*. Oxford: Oxford University Press.

Frost, M. (1986). *Towards a normative theory of international relations*. Cambridge: Cambridge University Press.

Frost, M. (1996). *Ethics in international relations: A constitutive theory*. Cambridge: Cambridge University Press.

Frost, M. (2002). *Constituting human rights: Global civil society and the society of democratic states*. London: Routledge.

Fukuyama, F. (1992). *The end of history and the last man*. New York: Free Press.

Geldenhuys, D. (1990). *Isolated states*. Johannesburg: Jonathan Ball.

Hegel, G. (1973a). *The philosophy of right*. (T. M. Knox). Oxford: Oxford University Press.

Hegel, G. (1973b). *The philosophy of right*. (T. M. Knox). Oxford: Oxford University Press.

Held, D., & McClure, N. (2000). *The global transformation reader*. Cambridge: Polity Press.

Holzgrefe, J., & Keohane, R. O. (eds). (2003). *Humanitarian intervention: Ethical, legal and political dilemmas*. Cambridge: Cambridge University Press.

Huntington, S. (1996). *The clash of civilisations and the making of the new order*. New York: Simon and Shuster.

Jabri, V. (2007, March). Michel Foucault's analytics of war: The social, the international, and the racial. *International Political Sociology, 1*(1), 67–82.

Jackson, R. (1990). *Quasi-states: Sovereignty, international relations and the Third World*. Cambridge: Cambridge University Press.

Krasner, S. D. (1995, Winter). Compromising Westphalia. *International Security, 20*(3), 115–151.

Laidi, Z. (1998). *A world without meaning – the crisis of meaning in international politics*. London: Routledge.

Lapid, Y., & Kratochwil, F. (eds). (1996). *The return of culture and identity in international relations theory*. Boulder: Lynne Rienner.

Lebow, R., Ned. (2003). *The tragic vision of politics: Ethics, interests and orders*. Cambridge: Cambridge University Press.

Lenin, V. (1977). Imperialism, the highest stage of capitalism. In *Selected Works of Lenin*. Moscow: Progress Publishers.

Linklater, A. (1990). The problem of community in international relations. *Alternatives: Social Transformation and Humane Governance, 15*(2), 135–153.

Linklater, A. (1998). *The transformation of political community*. Cambridge: Polity Press.

Locke, J. (1952). *The second treatise of government*. Indianapolis: Bobbs-Merrill.

Lukes, S. (1974). *Power: A radical view*. London: Macmillan.

Mearsheimer, J. (2001). *The tragedy of great power politics*. New York: Norton.

Mulhall, S., & Swift, A. (1992). *Liberals and communitarians*. Oxford: Blackwell.

Nardin, T. (1983). *Law morality and relations of states*. Princeton, N.J.: Princeton University Press.

Nicolson, H. (1961). *The old diplomacy and the new*. David Davies Memorial Institute of International Studies.

Nozick, R. (1974). *Anarchy, state and utopia*. Oxford: Blackwell.

Parris, M. (2006). *I should welcome the Baker Report, so why do I feel sick?* [Column]. London: *The Times*.

Paskins, B., & Dockrill, M. (1979). *The Ethics of War*. London: Duckworth.

Polanyi, K. (1957). *The great transformation*. Boston: Beacon Press.

Rawls, J. (1993). The law of peoples. In S. Shute & S. Hurley (eds), *On human rights* (pp. 41–82). New York, NY: Basic Books.

Raz, J. (1986). *The morality of freedom*. Oxford: Oxford University Press.

Schatzki, T. R. (1996). *Social practices: A Wittgensteinian approach to human activity and the social*. Cambridge: Cambridge University Press.

Schmidt, B. C. (2004). Realism as tragedy. *Review of International Studies, 30*(3), 427–441.

Shaw, M. (1994). *Global society and international relations*. Cambridge: Cambridge University Press.

Shaw, M. (ed.). (1999). *Politics and globalisation: Knowledge, ethics and agency*. London: Routledge.

Spirtas, M. (1996). A house divided: Tragedy and evil in realist theory. In B. Frankel, *Realism: Restatements and renewal*. London: Frank Cass.

Stopford, J., & Strange, S. (1991). *Rival states rival firms: Competition for world market shares*. Cambridge: Cambridge University Press.

Time Magazine. (2006, Saturday 9th December). Iraq foreign minister offers USA support in Iraq.

Waltz, K. (1979). *Theory of international politics*. London: Addison-Wesley.

Walzer, M. (1980). The moral standing of states: A reply to four critics. *Philosophy and Public Affairs, IX*.

Walzer, M. (1994). *Thick and thin: Moral argument at home and abroad*. Notre Dame: University of Notre Dame Press.

Wendt, A. (1992). Anarchy is what states make of it: The social construction of power politics. *International Organization, 46*(2).

Wight, M. (1979). *Power politics*. Harmondsworth: Penguin Books.

INDEX